W9-AWM-835

WHERE DEATH AND GLORY MEET

Where Death and Glory Meet

Colonel Robert Gould Shaw

AND THE

54th Massachusetts Infantry

RUSSELL DUNCAN

The University of Georgia Press | Athens and London

© 1999 by the University of Georgia Press
Athens, Georgia 30602
All rights reserved
Designed by Erin Kirk New
Set in 11 on 14 Monotype Walbaum by G & S Typesetters, Inc.

Printed in the United States of America

ISBN 0-8203-2135-4

*Frontispiece: Colonel Robert Gould Shaw, Fifty-fourth
Massachusetts Infantry, May 1863. Boston Athenaeum.*

Here is her witness: this, her perfect son,
This delicate and proud New England soul
Who leads despised men, with just-unshackled feet,
Up the large ways where death and glory meet.

WILLIAM VAUGHN MOODY,
"An Ode in Time of Hesitation"

FOR BONNIE

CONTENTS

PREFACE

ROBERT GOULD SHAW was merely a competent officer, but he was not an ordinary soldier. Coming from great wealth and advantage, Shaw stood among the high-profile regiments of the war: Seventh New York National Guard, Second Massachusetts Infantry, and Fifty-fourth Massachusetts (Colored) Infantry. The Seventh distinguished itself by being the first regiment to arrive in Washington after Lincoln's call for troops. The Second was Boston's own, and many Brahmin sons officered its men. The Fifty-fourth, the vanguard unit that became the most watched regiment of the war, filled its ranks with the cream of the Northern black population. Shaw joined to fight for the North, to do his duty, and to prove his courage and manhood. In that, he was a very average soldier. But he was also a man on the cusp—coming of age—posing and pondering questions about the meaning of the war and the ever narrowing and widening gap between his expectations of national honor and the reality of killing countrymen.

Shaw's letters home—from which this biography is overwhelmingly drawn—convey the change wrought by battlefield casualties, camp life, commitment, and homesickness upon the sensibilities of youth. His soldiering experience was as common as it was distinctive. He joined to win a quick war but committed to fight to the end. He "saw the elephant" at Cedar Mountain, Antietam, and Fort Wagner, made wearying marches, and spent days in tedious boredom awaiting orders to the front, orders to anywhere. Like others, he wanted wounds—and got them. The adrenaline of life and death on the field of battle brought Shaw closer to his comrades in a male world than he had ever been to his classmates at Harvard or to his boyhood companions. This universe of maleness helped him to pull at the strings of his female-dominated family, and helped him mature even though he had not been able to break free of his mother's dominance by the time of his death. In that sense Shaw never got past his mother. The famous monument on Boston Common—which is widely regarded as the finest bronze and marble monument commemorating the Civil War—is much more representative of her ambition than of his.

Shaw's life helps illuminate the pressures heaped on a son brought up in an antislavery community infused with ideas of *noblesse oblige*, while it conveys the wrenching struggle of a boyman trying to make sense of a war among brothers. Shaw's elaborately privileged education and influential family connections gave him the training and language to express himself by writing. His prose is often eloquent, always articulate, intensely informative, amusing, heartwrenching, and provocative, more than a century after he described himself and his times to his family and friends.

This biography is stronger because of Shaw's trustworthiness about his own misdirections, camp conditions, and battle maneuvers. After his father published excerpts from his August 12, 1862, letter home in the aftermath of the battle of Cedar Mountain, Shaw warned, "I can't write what I want to, if my letters are to be put in the papers." Shaw's family kept subsequent correspondence private until after his death. In return they received honest accounts of his experiences and sincere expressions of his thoughts. We too, then, are privy to his celebration of life in an environment of death.[1]

Shaw's experience in the war is a microcosm of the conflict. Within a week of Fort Sumter, he marched into Washington and swore before Lincoln that he would fight for the Union. Three months later, after training at Brook Farm, he was striding into

Harper's Ferry singing "John Brown's Body" and beginning to reflect that the war was about more than nationhood. After his friends and fellows began to die, Shaw grew into a competent officer and into a man who hoped that the higher goal of freedom could be achieved by a Northern victory.

Cedar Mountain brought the destructive war to Shaw in the form of Stonewall Jackson's assault and victory. Positioned in a wheatfield, Shaw's Second Infantry lost sixteen of its twenty-three officers killed or wounded. Before Shaw came fully to grips with the suffering that resulted from this Virginia battle, he fought through a bloodier slaughter in a Maryland cornfield along meandering Antietam Creek. With more officers dead and the regiment at half strength, Shaw knew firsthand the costs of war.

Although he never found himself in the worlds of scholars, reformers, or businessmen, this short, blond, small-boned, blue-eyed youth discovered himself among the living and dead soldiers of war. A boy who could not adapt to the discipline in civilian circles became a good soldier who followed orders and expected the same from others. He could be counted on when bullets flew and Rebels yelled. Twice wounded, he proved himself in the grim battle of Antietam in September 1862. He wrote hundreds of letters home, and they are significantly devoid of homesick whining. Shaw stood up to be counted, and he intended to see the war to conclusion or death. Then he finally got "big inside" and courageous enough to do the bravest thing he ever did, accepting the command of the North's first regiment of black soldiers, the Fifty-fourth. He became a reformer, whether he liked it or not.

The preliminary, then the actual, Emancipation Proclamation replaced the goal of Union with the higher one of Freedom and thereby lifted the Civil War to a moral plane that makes it worth studying and teaching. Black men enlisted as soldiers to end slavery and to prove themselves capable of citizenship. Shaw is important to history only because of his position atop the North's first black regiment and because of the symbolism inherent in the monument on Boston Common. In fact, Shaw became the most important abolitionist hero of the war; there is none greater. Before the war John Brown had fulfilled this role; but during the war it was Shaw who became, in the words of William James, "a great symbol of deeper things than he ever realized himself." He also won the monument on Boston Common and the poems of the Lowells and others. When Shaw accepted the colonelcy of the Fifth-fourth Massachusetts Infantry and led it past the ditches and abattis to die and kill on the parapets of Fort Wagner, part of the Charleston Harbor defenses, he gave us an education: in race relations, in strength of character, and in the meaning of freedom in his times—and in ours.[2]

I want to thank the friends, family, colleagues, and strangers who supported me through the many days of research and writing. This book could not have been completed without hours spent sitting by the fire, working in the classroom, and discussing materials that make up deadlines of publication and daily life.

This is how the book came to be: after he read the manuscript pages of my introduction to the published letters of Robert Gould Shaw, *Blue-Eyed Child of Fortune* (1992), William McFeely encouraged me to expand that short biography into a book of its own. Book reviewers seemed to agree with him. In the *New York Times Book Review*, for example, Harold Holzer concluded that my "introductory essay . . . may be the best life story yet written about the young hero." Because Shaw deserved more than an "introduction," this book found print.

Malcolm Call helped me find my voice, again. Karen Orchard and the staff of the University of Georgia Press, especially Kristine Blakeslee and Erin Hoge, smoothed the rough spots in the publication process. Ellen Harris used her quick eye and judgment to copyedit the manuscript.

Clara Juncker did many things to make life full while making room for the writing. Our two-year conversation immensely bettered this biography. Maria, Eva, and Anna sometimes danced and played on tiptoes so that paragraphs might become pages. From a group of possible titles, Bonnie selected the one most likely to make her "want to read the book." When Clara and Malcolm agreed with her choice—for the reason that it was "right"—I decided that the dedication to Bonnie had been prearranged. Perhaps my working title, "Drumbeat of the Common Heart," is best placed here, for Bonnie.

1 Boston Common

ON THE BOSTON COMMON, Robert Gould Shaw rides his horse in step with his regiment marching southward forever with straight backs, forward eyes, and long strides. In Augustus Saint-Gaudens's greatest sculpture, Shaw, white, and his men, black—and all bronze—recall that eight-and-twentieth day of May in 1863, when one thousand men strode with swaying steps and swinging flags through the streets of Boston and into glory. The drummer boys tapped out the beat, and the men's voices sang out their vow that while John Brown's body might be a-mould'ring in the grave, they would carry forward his vision of black men redeeming themselves from 250 years of slavery. In their right hands and on their right shoulders gleamed a thousand Enfield rifles that had been supplied them from an armory they had not had to break open to obtain.[1]

The largest crowd in the city's history assembled on Essex and Beacon Streets, leaned from balconies, waved from windows, ran out to touch or praise, and surrounded the reviewing stands around the State House and in the Common to cheer and gape at the pride of abolitionist Boston. Hundreds of wives and sweethearts smiled and fretted over their men. Frederick Douglass, a formidable man in stature, stood even taller and bigger as he watched his eldest son, Lewis, march past. Douglass surely recalled his own words as he saw each black soldier with "an eagle on his button and a musket on his shoulder" and was sure that this would earn them "the right to citizenship in the United States." William Lloyd Garrison wept openly as he rested against a bust of John Brown at Wendell Phillips's home overlooking the parade route. John Greenleaf Whittier, a pacifist who attended the parade of no other unit for fear that doing so would encourage and give "a new impulse to war," could not keep away from the line of march. Thomas Sims—a runaway slave who had been dragged from Boston back to Georgia in 1861 under the Fugitive Slave Act, sold downriver to Mississippi, and finally freed in 1863—trembled happily as he saw armed black men conquering the same ground on which he had been chained and returned to bondage. The family of Colonel Shaw, commander of the Fifty-fourth Massachusetts Infantry, watched and hugged one another as their son, brother, and husband saluted them by briefly stopping his horse and raising his sword to his lips in front of the house at 44 Beacon Street. When this day passed, they would see his youthful figure again only when the statue found its place on the Common in 1897.[2]

Sixty years before the unveiling, Shaw was born into one of the nation's richest families. He had all the advantages of the fortunate—the easy life, famous friends, best schools, finest clothes, widest travels, ripest food, and richest drink the world could offer. Yet he died with sand in his mouth and sword in hand, face down among the sons of the unfortunate and despised. Shaw never attained the scholarly insight of his father, the reform conviction of his mother and sisters, or the business acumen of his grandfathers and uncles. He did not join the army in 1861 to fight for the Union or to free the slaves, but simply to do his duty. He did want to avenge the name of his country and to revenge what he considered years of bullying by Southern slaveholders. He did not particularly care if the South was forced back into the Union; he had merely grown tired of the atmosphere of sectional tension that pervaded his daily life. Shaw craved a nation freed from this disorderly opprobrium so that he could get on with the pleasures of living. Eight hundred days of war barely changed his outlook before it spilled his lifeblood into the sand of South Carolina. Friends and family, poets and philosophers, Northerners and Southerners, and blacks and whites eventually would praise him and make him a martyr to a cause he neither fully understood nor dedicated himself to.

 Brahmin Childhood

BORN IN BOSTON on October 10, 1837, when his mother was twenty-two years old and his father twenty-eight, Shaw grew familiar with nannies, housekeepers, and servants attendant to children of his social standing. Education held a high place in his parents' understanding of individual perfection and in the attainments necessary to male heirs, and so Shaw found himself often around tutors and classrooms. After learning his alphabet and doing early reading at home, Shaw attended an "infant's school" before being sent to the kindergarten of Miss Mary Peabody.[1]

But childhood is more than school—even in Puritan-based Massachusetts. Shaw played with his older sister, Anna, and younger sisters, Susanna, Josephine, and Ellen, in the homes of his many uncles and aunts. His father, Francis George Shaw, was the eldest of eleven children, and his mother, Sarah Blake Sturgis Shaw, stood eighth in a brood of twelve. Robert's eighty-five first cousins afforded him plenty of playmates. As was and is the custom among the gentry, the children of his parents' friends were among his first and most lasting acquaintances, being willing confederates whenever the Shaws visited. Willie and George Garrison often played with Robert in the house and garden of their father, the abolitionist editor of the *Liberator*, William Lloyd Garrison. In Garrison's home Robert listened to, and was often bored by, the adults' never-ending discussions about the immorality of human bondage. Garrison and the Shaws early entered the contest to out-law slavery and remained consistent benefactors to the cause of freedom. Years after their father died, Willie and George Garrison remembered the Shaws among "the original abolitionists."[2]

Robert's grandfathers, Robert Gould Shaw and Nathaniel Russell Sturgis, made millions of dollars in the West India and China importing trades of their fathers. The first Robert Shaw, born on June 4, 1776, was Boston's wealthiest merchant, operating a dry-goods store, an auction and commission house, and a real-estate business, together worth $1.5 million in 1852. He was of paramount importance in the rise of Boston economic power in the nineteenth century. As Shaws intermarried with Sturgises and others, the variously named companies of Russell and Sturgis, Russell and Company, and Sturgis, Shaw and Company opened offices in Boston, Manila, Canton, and New York City and made or increased the fortunes of many relatives, including the families Cabot, Forbes, Russell, Parkman, Hunnewell, and Lodge. Obviously, the extended family succeeded at business. Francis Shaw admired his father's work ethic, describing him as "a real merchant, loving business for its own sake."[3]

But Francis believed and often said that commerce had become "Mammon, the great god of our incomplete civilization." He loved ideas more, and so in 1841 the thirty-one-year-old Francis retired from his occupation as a merchant and part-time lawyer and moved his family to West Roxbury, Massachusetts, neighboring the newly established commune of Brook Farm. He had helped create the commune by bankrolling the founder, George Ripley. Nathaniel Hawthorne, a Brook Farm participant, remembered Shaw's monetary contributions as crucial but insisted his goodwill and humanitarianism were more important than money. In this brief, and idyllic, noncommercial world, Shaw devoted the rest of his life to literary pursuits, family, and philanthropy. He translated many fictional and historical works into English, including George

Sand's *Consuelo* (1848) and Heinrich Zschokke's *History of Switzerland* (1855).[4]

Shaw allied himself with those who wanted to raise the lot of the working class. He rejected the idea that the overall advancement of society required some people to be poor. He also scoffed at the notion that poverty was a permanent condition and refused to believe in a hierarchy of races. The responsibility to better the world must be shouldered. One of his closest friends recalled that Shaw "believed too much in man to accept the state of things as the will of God." Shaw believed in, translated, and published the socialist views of Mathieu Briancourt's *The Organization of Labor and Association* (1847) and Felix Cantegrel's *The Children of the Phalanstery* (1848). To give wider audience to the ideals of a happier social order, he put into English Charles Pellarin's *The Life of Charles Fourier* (1848). Many of Shaw's translations first appeared in the Brook Farm paper, the *Harbinger.*[5]

Later he wrote "A Piece of Land," which reformer Henry George included in his famous work *Social Problems* (1883)—a book dedicated to Shaw. Shaw cast "A Piece of Land" as a morality play with three characters: Labor, Capital, and Landowner. Labor leased Capital's spade to plant a potato crop for market on common land. At harvest time Labor paid for his use of the spade with interest in the form of a share of the crop. All was fine and good as Capital and Labor became partners. Labor rose and prospered. Then the villain Landowner stepped in, put up fences, and charged Labor exorbitant prices, which soon drove Labor and his family into the ruin of the poorhouse. All society suffered from the greed of Landowner. The play expounded the tenets of free-labor ideology as well as George's repugnance at the power that went with the ownership of land. Shaw promoted fairness to all groups and worried over what the inequities of class and race portended for the future.[6]

The Shaws did not join fully in the communal lifestyle at Brook

Farm, but they associated weekly with many of that group of intellectuals and reformers, including Ralph Waldo Emerson, Nathaniel Hawthorne, and Margaret Fuller. Francis and his wife's
brother-in-law George Russell, who had retired at age thirty-five
and also lived in West Roxbury, had helped finance the startup
costs of Brook Farm. They continued to provide monetary support
until the experiment ended in 1847. Unitarians made up a large
number of the communalists and came under the direct influence
of ministers William Channing and Theodore Parker. Parker had
a small country church near Brook Farm where he preached abolitionism, rational thinking, openmindedness, and human uplift.
He told his congregation that man had to expand beyond "self-
culture," not only to improve the individual but also to rid the
nation of social problems and injustice to better the entire "house."
The Shaws regularly attended Parker's services and counted him
among their close friends.[7]

3 Abolitionist Upbringing

ROBERT ATTENDED SCHOOL in West Roxbury and was influ-
enced by the humanitarianism of the Brook Farm intellectuals.
His father and mother were devoted to the antislavery cause, and
the boy knew not only William Lloyd Garrison but also other
friends of the family, including Harriet Beecher Stowe. Sarah
Shaw's closest friend and lifelong correspondent was Lydia Maria
Child. Child began writing in favor of abolition in 1833 with "An
Appeal in Favour of That Class of Americans Called Africans," and
from 1840 to 1844 she and her husband, David, coedited the *Anti-
Slavery Standard.* Her widely published 1859 edition of letters between John Brown and Governor Henry Wise of Virginia fueled
the controversy over slavery, helped make Brown a martyr, and

provided a strongly worded argument that the North was under the heel of the Southern aristocracy and "Slave Power." Child and Sarah Shaw attended classes together at Brook Farm and strengthened each other in the face of those who wanted abolitionists and women to keep quiet. The young Robert, often at his mother's knee, listened intently and wondered why slavery caused such passion in the women who inhabited his world. Few children in nineteenth-century America had stronger feminist role models than young Shaw.[1]

Shaw's parents joined Child in the American Anti-Slavery Society in 1838, and by 1842 Francis was working with the Boston Vigilance Committee to help runaway slaves to freedom. That same year, Francis, with Wendell Phillips and five others, headed a petition drive asking Congress for the immediate abolition of slavery and the slave trade in the District of Columbia. The petition called this request "a question of justice" and asked that no new states be admitted to the Union whose constitutions tolerated slavery. In 1851, Vigilance Committee members unsuccessfully tried to rescue Thomas Sims from the slave catchers; their failure only increased their conviction to oppose the Fugitive Slave Law.[2]

The abolitionists clung to one another for the support necessary to carry on with their convictions. One of Francis Shaw's best friends, Sydney Howard Gay, who edited the *Anti-Slavery Standard* before becoming managing editor of the *New York Tribune* in 1862, observed that this small group of reformers seemed "to the outside world a set of pestilent fanatics . . . [but were] among themselves the most charming circle of cultivated men and women that it has ever been my lot to know." The Shaws consistently devoted their time, money, and influence to gain freedom for slaves. One neighbor said of Francis, "He was a man among ten thousand. Born to wealth, he treated his wealth very largely as a trust for the use and benefit of suffering mankind. To every good cause he lent his sympathy, his advocacy, and his material support."[3]

So it was with those who clung to the Unitarian church. The first Robert Shaw and his wife, Elizabeth Parkman, relieved themselves of the sterner tenets of Boston Puritanism to accept religious instruction as Unitarians. Capitalism and good works combined into a religion of the heart and head taught from the pulpit of the Federal Street Church by William Ellery Channing. Francis and Sarah grew up in the weekly services and developed a Brahmin conscience of civic responsibility as salvation and progressive community. The children—Robert and his sisters—were schooled upon the foundations of Puritan Boston, trimmed up by Unitarianism beliefs of service, shaken by the transcendentalism of Brook Farm, and benefited by their social station in the most elite circles of American society.[4]

 Jesuit Education

WHEN BROOK FARM declined and his wife's eyesight began to fail, Shaw moved the family to Staten Island to be near the nation's premier eye specialist, Samuel MacKenzie Elliott. The Shaws settled in the fashionable north end resort town of West New Brighton, a literary neighborhood of Unitarians, Free-Soilers, and abolitionists. They interacted with other patients of Elliott—including Francis Parkman, Henry David Longfellow, Charles Dana, and George Ripley—as well as neighbors and visitors like Sydney Howard Gay, Ralph Waldo Emerson, Lydia Maria Child, James Russell Lowell, and a constellation of other activists. The Shaws often took the ferry to Brooklyn to attend the church of Henry Ward Beecher and were instrumental in establishing a Unitarian church on Staten Island.[1]

The island was a sparsely settled rural area of fourteen thousand residents, and nine-year-old Robert found the island a wonder to be explored. On the North Shore, farmland interplayed with dense woods near the mouth of the Kills, where a deep ravine extended inland and accepted the ebb and flow of the tide. Robert picked ripe blackberries and explored this mysterious terrain with his sisters. He often ran with his dogs, Rover and Argus, up through the open fields of high grass down to the banks of the river. To secure his education, Sarah placed him in the private school of "Herr Marschalk."[2]

When the time came for Robert to advance to more challenging studies—at age thirteen—his uncle Coolidge Shaw miraculously talked Francis and Sarah into sending the boy to the preparatory school of Saint John's College in Fordham, New York. Probably the Shaws thought that an "inside" knowledge of Catholicism would only further their son's education. Uncle Coolidge had forsaken material goods to join the Jesuits and felt that a Catholic schooling would be good intellectual discipline for his nephew.[3]

Robert's first letter to his mother in June 1850 revealed his response to being away from home, to the workload, and to the discipline: "I wish you hadn't sent me here while you are on the island, because I want to be there, and now I have to stay at this old place. I'm sure I shan't want to come here after vacation for I hate it like everything." In September, Robert continued his litany of "I hate Fordham" and added a note about his professor: "My old Teacher scolded me to-day because I didn't do something he didn't tell me to do, and I hate him." He confided that his homesickness embarrassed him when he cried in front of his classmates. There is no evidence that he was punished by "Father Regnier, the one who whips the boys," but he ran away twice and told his parents in October, "I'd rather do anything than stay here."[4]

Nevertheless, he remained at Fordham for the entire semester, rising at 5:30 "in the cold and dark" to begin a rigorous schooling under serious men. He studied French, Spanish, Latin, and Greek, and continued his violin lessons. He kept up a regular correspondence with his parents, a habit that would continue throughout his life. His mother had insisted upon it, even though Robert often complained, "I don't want to write every week; it's too much trouble." Showing a youthful egocentrism, Robert added, "I shall only write when I want something."[5]

Because thirteen-year-olds nearly always have something they want, Robert wrote very regularly. He asked for an accordion this time, a dictionary that time, the "Waverley Novels" another, a pocket watch in another, and, once, "a strong and pretty large knife." And always Robert confided that he missed home. He often plotted to run away or to take a trip to Boston or elsewhere. He was sensitive to criticism and often chafed when he believed that he had been unjustly disciplined for — or accused of — breaches of conduct. He could be counted on to remark, "It wasn't my fault" — and he fixed the blame on unruly boys or unbending priests.[6]

While Robert attended school, his parents planned an extended tour of Europe. Sarah's eyesight had improved, and the intellectual Margaret Fuller, a family friend, encouraged Sarah to join her in Europe, imploring, "Come with all your children and live quietly here!" In the growing tradition of the "grand tour," established by their friends — including the James family — the Shaws decided that four years abroad would improve their spirits and knowledge. A European tour had become a mandatory part of a nineteenth-century aristocratic education; the Shaws also used the occasion to begin the construction of a new house. In January 1851 they collected Robert, said goodbye to Fordham forever, and sailed in first-class accommodations from New York. After a summer of touring in France and Switzerland, Robert found himself again in a boarding school while his sisters stayed with the family, being educated at home.[7]

5 Neuchâtel

FOR THE NEXT five years Robert studied, developed a "wander-lust" he never lost, and lived through those particularly difficult years between the ages of thirteen and eighteen. Beginning in October, he attended the boarding school of Monsieur and Madame Roulet in Neuchâtel, Switzerland. He could hardly have found a more beautiful setting. Neuchâtel sits on the western edge of a lake cradled by the Jura Mountains, in the western part of the country near the border with France. Shaw looked southward from his corner room up the valley to the magnificent, rounded, snow-covered form of Mont Blanc. His southeastern vista brought the Alpine peaks of the Jungfrau and Eiger pressing into his window. In summer, orchestras played in the town park, and grapes grew spectacularly big and sugar-rich to be turned into the wine Shaw learned to love. Still, Shaw missed his parents. While pleased that "M. and Mme. Roulet are very kind," he still felt he had been "left" and wrote, "I hate to be here. I keep thinking what you are all doing." Shaw would never outgrow his need to be with his family or his special love for his mother, who remained his faithful confidant until his death. He did, however, learn to like Mr. Roulet as a friend and came to enjoy Neuchâtel.[1]

Roulet administered a rigorous curriculum. Shaw studied geometry, algebra, chemistry, and geology as well as six languages—though he concentrated on French and German. Switzerland is a geographical crossroads for languages, and students can hardly find a better place to hear and study a variety of tongues. Shaw took parts in student theater productions and kept up his lessons in violin and piano. In good weather Roulet took the students on tours in France and Switzerland, teaching as he went. Roulet believed in and emphasized a nurturing of the students, but he could lose his temper over breaches in discipline. As Shaw told his mother, "Roulet hardly ever gets mad about the lessons, but only when we break some of the rules, or are impolite. But when he does get angry he's just like the wolf." Still, Shaw never saw the master punish anyone; rather, "he only scolds." Shaw did resent having to explain where and when and why every time he wanted to go for a walk or take a horseback ride or visit town. After a year of explanations, Shaw remarked, "I shall be very glad to have more freedom when I leave here.[2]

During his two years at Neuchâtel, Shaw struggled to define himself and the world around him. He had grown up among ardent abolitionists; now he began to evaluate whether he could live up to the level of his parents' dedication to social reform. His self-searching coincided with the release of Harriet Beecher Stowe's *Uncle Tom's Cabin* (1852), which Shaw read and reread. He perused newspaper articles about Southern slavery and Northern compliance with the Fugitive Slave Law and reported, "I didn't know there were a great many free blacks in our slaveholding States." He questioned his parents about comparative statistics concerning numbers of blacks and whites in the South. In many of his letters Shaw fished for his parents' opinions by mentioning *Uncle Tom* or slavery. His mother wrote him that Mrs. Stowe was the sister of Henry Ward Beecher, the minister in Brooklyn whom she liked so much, and that Stowe had written the novel "as a matter of conscience, after the passage of the 'Fugitive Slave Law.'" Shaw responded that he hoped Russians would read the novel and that it would "help them to set their slaves free." He questioned whether the royalists in Rome would ban the book because of its republican principles. Still, in a worldly teenage reflection, he resigned himself to the status quo and rationalized, "I don't see how one man could do much against slavery." Earlier, he made his position clear: "I don't want to become reformer, Apostle, or anything of that kind." Yet when Stowe's *The Key to Uncle Tom's Cabin* (1853) was published, Shaw pored through it for the "facts" of slavery.[3]

Shaw also questioned religion. He never forgave the Jesuits for his experience at Fordham. After he received a letter from one of his Saint John's teacher-priests who feared for his education at Roulet's and expressed the hope that Robert would go to school in Italy, Shaw scoffed: "He meant that he's afraid I won't be converted to Catholicism, because he hopes I'd be left in the clutches of the Jesuits at Rome, and would become Catholic right off." On the other hand, Shaw did his best to hide his Unitarian upbringing from everyone, because to mention it "would only bring up discussions and conversations which would be very stupid and tiresome." When Roulet tried to convince Shaw that he should take religion classes and attend church regularly, Shaw angrily wrote his parents that it was not Roulet's business if he were "good or bad" and that those students who do go are not "any better than me and that's what I told them." Shaw, who would never devote himself to a church or to a religion as his parents did, did attend Protestant worship services of several denominations.[4]

Shaw also began to look at career goals. He did not want to be a reformer, which was the occupation—or rather calling—of both his parents, but what did he want? Education surely, but where? His father had gone to Harvard, so that became the likely choice. He mentioned Harvard to his parents in one sentence and in the next probably caused them a little concern by announcing, "I think I should like to go to West Point." His parents probably laughed at and worried about this; with their son's loathing of discipline and authority, the army seemed the least likely place for him to succeed and as far from their pacific concerns as any institution could be. After Sarah wrote him of her disapproval of his military leanings, Shaw insisted, "I think I should like it, and what else can I do? I can't think of any thing else, for I don't want to be a Merchant, or Doctor, or Minister, or any thing like that." In his early teens, Shaw still had plenty of time to reconsider his prospects.[5]

6 Hanover

DURING THE SUMMER of 1853, Shaw traveled with Roulet throughout Switzerland and said goodbye to him as school began again in September. He had not seen his mother or sisters for over a year and had had only one visit from his father, who was on his way to Boston for the funeral of his own father. Robert spent the next ten months reunited with his family at their rented house in Sorrento on the Amalfi peninsula south of Naples. The sun was hot and constant, and the languages Italian and English. The family used the house as a comfortable base while they toured Rome, Florence, and Heidelberg. They often entertained old friends or greeted new ones. In Sorrento the Shaws met and hosted the famous English actress Frances "Fanny" Kemble, an abolitionist who had been married to Pierce Butler, the wealthiest slaveowner along Georgia's rice coast. Kemble held the Shaws spellbound with stories about her firsthand experiences among the slaves. She certainly must have answered questions from Shaw, as he compared what she knew with what he had read in *Uncle Tom's Cabin*. A decade after they sat among the grapevines and rocky shoreline of Sorrento, Shaw would find himself on the very plantation Kemble described to him.[1]

After celebrating the Fourth of July with his parents and sisters, Shaw, accompanied by his father, traveled north to Hanover, Germany, where they secured him "two rooms—a parlour and a bedroom" in the home of Herr and Frau Eisendecher and their two daughters. Servants cleaned his room and served elaborate meals.

Besides breakfast in the parlor and lunch in the dining room, daily at four o'clock Shaw took coffee in the garden. Evenings at eight, he dined on "a great big supper upstairs." He was privately educated in Hanover for the next two years, hiring tutors to further his classical education. He remained concerned about slavery and about his own future but spent most of his time pursuing pleasure. After all, he had not yet turned sixteen, his parents were far away, no Jesuit watched his every move, and Monsieur Roulet was in Switzerland demanding explanations from other boys. Independent for the first time, Shaw made his own schedule and used his own house key to let himself in or out whenever he chose. Recognizing his relative lack of homesickness, Shaw wrote his mother of "how big inside I've got since I've been here. I'm at least five years older than when I came." [2]

His mother probably wondered how "big" he had gotten when she read in his letter of November 5: "I have no taste for anything excepting amusing myself!" He had spent all his money and, in a statement that must have seemed arrogant to Sarah, said, "You mention my becoming a merchant, but that is entirely out of the question. I had rather be a chimney-sweep." Eight months later, Shaw told his mother, "I hope that when I come home I shall be as much at liberty as I am now for after having had my own way as much as if I were of age for two years it would be nasty to be a child again. It's very unwillingly that I ask you to let me do anything because that's submission, but I haven't enough money to do it otherwise." [3]

Despite his boasts and threats, Shaw managed to give time to his studies, from 9:00 A.M. to 2:00 P.M. daily, with an occasional late afternoon class. Most nights he was in place for the 7:00 curtain at the theater, opera, or concert. He loved literature and music. Shakespeare enchanted him; he saw *A Midsummer Night's Dream* eight times and *Hamlet* twice. Shaw attended many performances of operatic and symphonic pieces, among them *The Barber of Se-*

ville, The Marriage of Figaro, The Magic Flute, Don Giovanni, Othello, William Tell, and several of Beethoven's works.[4]

He became a regular at parties. At a "fancy-ball" in February 1855, Shaw shaved his blond beard and dressed as a woman. He had reached his full height of five feet five inches, was slim, and had delicate features. Looking much like his sisters Anna and Josephine, he "made such fools" of his friends, none of whom recognized him until he spoke. At the party he drank too much champagne. The next night he attended a ball that started at seven and ended at six the next morning, and left him feeling "rather seedy . . . as it's almost impossible not to drink a good deal, because there is so much good wine here." It had taken him a little over a year to throw off a previous announcement: "I shouldn't like to get into the habit of drinking much wine and beer"—but then, of course, a seventeen-year-old is light years advanced from a fifteen-year-old.[5]

As he got bolder with his freedom, he took a two-month-long trip to Norway with two other students from Hanover, informing his parents of it only after he returned. Not surprisingly, he complained, "My purse is getting hollow cheeks again." When his mother counseled him against "sprees," Shaw countered that he was enjoying his youth. When she wrote of his spendthrift ways, Shaw bristled, "I have not been very extravagant," and told his father, "I think Mother's letter is a bit too strong." Actually his mother had miscalculated his expenses by 120 English pounds and quickly apologized to her son. Patronizingly, Shaw replied to his mother, "I won't be too hard upon you . . . your excuse is ample satisfaction."[6]

In the midst of his pleasure, Shaw turned his attention away from slavery. He did mention the formation of a new abolitionist society in New York. He took notice of a *Tribune* account of a slave's being burned alive in Alabama and commented, "I didn't think that this . . . would happen again." Beyond those brief mentions, which may have been included to pacify his mother, Shaw does not appear to have given much thought to abolition. There is no mention of the Kansas-Nebraska Act or of the sensational stories about "Bleeding Kansas." Shaw's letters are filled to overflowing with tales of travels to Berlin, Paris, and Norway, party escapades, crushes on women, and despair that he is not "growing any more." His mother could take a Janus-like consolation in her son's confession that there were fifteen English girls boarding in Hanover and that, because they went to church every Sunday, "I am beginning to go too." [7]

Besides his growing curiosity about women and drink, the only real emotion in Shaw's European letters to his family came bursting forth on December 11, 1855. At a tea party Shaw met a man who "railed against America." Shaw admitted, "I did get very angry to-night. I can't help wishing for war between America and some European country, and that I were in the navy, so that I might cut some of their heads open. . . . I must hate them when they talk so about us; and the worst of it is, that they don't say anything against the real abuse, Slavery, but begin on some little insignificant thing. . . . They generally talk of the Know-nothings and the bullying of emigrants. But whatever anybody says about America here commonly puts me in a wax." [8]

Shaw maintained this strong sense of national patriotism throughout his short life. As the years to civil war wound down, Shaw increasingly felt that what everyone called the Slave Power soiled the fabric of an otherwise great nation. When war came, he was primed to take revenge on the South for the abuse he had written about in December 1855. To him the South was the transgressor, not the North. If it took the end of slavery to redeem the honor of America and to end the embarrassment Northerners felt to be in the same union with an anachronistic system, then Shaw stood for that. If the North could avenge itself in battle against the South and then let it go with or without slavery intact, leaving the

North as a separate nation now more honorable for the fight, then Shaw stood for that. He never really felt the immorality of slavery the way the abolitionists did; he was never quite an abolitionist. His gripe with the Jesuits, Monsieur Roulet, his parents, and those who spoke against America certainly revolved around his struggle to become his own person, but it was more than that. When a priest disciplined, Roulet questioned, his parents scolded, or a foreigner opposed him, Shaw bristled and sought to right these "unfair" attacks on his honor. He demanded atonement. He would join the navy if he could "cut some of their heads open" and thus stop the offensive words coming from mouths of those who blasphemed his America. In 1861 he joined the army to do just that to Southerners. He would hope that slavery would fall, but he did not enlist to fight for that goal.

7 Harvard

EVEN WHILE HE TOLD his parents of his parties and travels and shared his feelings about girls, Shaw reassured them that his studies progressed well. He had decided on Harvard and thought that he would have no trouble passing the entrance examinations in the fall of 1856. He hoped he might be able to enter as a junior, but certainly would enter no lower than with sophomore standing. To help him—and perhaps being realistic about his academic abilities—his parents suggested that he might want a tutor to push him through an intensive study during the summer before he took the examinations. Coming to terms with his needs, Shaw acquiesced and told them, "Engage the Crammer by all means, and I'll work like a steam-engine when I get home."[1]

Shaw returned to Staten Island in May 1856 to much excitement. There was the newly finished eighty-thousand-dollar house on Bard Avenue in Elliotville. At least eight servants tended to the cooking, cleaning, driving, and gardening. Shaw liked the billiard room and often told stories of European adventures while he engaged friends in friendly competition. He met George William Curtis, a Brook Farmer who was well known as one of the country's top orators and writers and who edited *Putnam's Monthly.* Curtis, thirty-two, and Anna Shaw, twenty, were engaged and would marry that fall. In politics Shaw's father had been a vehement Free-Soiler and now contributed to the Republican party's first campaign. He had just returned from the Republican national convention, where he helped nominate John C. Frémont for president. Curtis made many speeches on behalf of the candidate. Frémont set up his New York campaign headquarters on Staten Island and attended the Shaw-Curtis wedding. At the same time, abolitionists were busy with lectures and weekly meetings at the neighboring house of Sydney Howard Gay, which became a refuge for runaway slaves. Prominent visitors to Gay's home included John Greenleaf Whittier, James Russell Lowell, Wendell Phillips, Angelina and Sarah Grimké, Robert Purvis, and Lucretia Mott. Meanwhile, Shaw spent long hours under the tutelage of the "Crammer," Francis C. Barlow, who had been educated at Brook Farm and graduated from Harvard as valedictorian; he became a general in the Civil War and the husband of Shaw's youngest sister, Ellen.[2]

Shaw passed the Harvard entrance examination, which he rated as "very easy." Yet he could enter only as a freshman. Taking up residence on campus, Shaw, spoiled by his elaborate European education, immediately found everything "horridly stupid here and just like a school." The freedom of Hanover did not repeat itself in American classrooms; he intensely disliked having "to ask when I want to go anywhere." By October, Shaw despaired of his preparation for Harvard's academic demands, even though he did speak and write fluently in German, Spanish, and French. He threatened to leave school to "go into a store" if "at the end of the year I stand very low." Shaw got his worst grades in mathematics and history. His dislike of discipline and his intellectual shortcomings brought the pronouncement, "I hate Cambridge." He considered transferring to Columbia or New York University but did not do so. Shaw stayed in school but never pulled himself academically into the top half of his class. He may have taken some consolation in the faculty's overall displeasure with the Class of 1860; he reported that the faculty felt "we are the laziest class they have had for a long while."[5]

Although he was academically challenged, Shaw excelled at extracurricular activities. He enjoyed playing "foot-ball," but with fifty to seventy men on a team all engaged at once, he was beaten up regularly by bigger players. He wrote that he had learned to keep "among fellows of my own size on the outskirts." His height made him feel inferior. After his trip to Norway in 1856, he had despaired "of growing any more." Asked to be one of four groomsmen in a wedding in 1858, Shaw complained to his mother, "I don't want to a bit. . . . The other three are all six feet tall." Some of his physical comparisons undoubtedly came from his sharing a room with Harvard's football and rowing champion, the tall and muscular Caspar Crowninshield. Shaw quickly quit football to participate in activities he felt better about. In his second year he joined a boat club and participated in rowing races with other clubs. He took boxing lessons. He played the violin well enough to join a musical group, the Pierians, who played twice a week. He was always inclined toward music and now wished often for even more musical talent. Undoubtedly, Shaw enjoyed the after-performance social hour of ale, cheese, and crackers. He was accepted into all eight societies sponsored by the university, although the Hasty Pudding Club, a theatrical organization, seemed reluctant to admit him. His best friend at Harvard was his cousin Harry

Russell, who combined ability and popularity to get elected president of many of the societies. Perhaps his wide-ranging activities strengthened his spirits and helped him past his height complex.[4]

During the time Shaw studied and played at Harvard, Boston and Cambridge buzzed constantly with abolitionist activities. Shaw was a visitor in the home of James Russell Lowell. He "escaped" school on the weekends by getting a pass to see his "guardian," Harry's father, George Russell, in West Roxbury. Every Sunday Russell took him to Theodore Parker's church, where they listened to Parker preach brilliantly against slavery and, on one occasion, heard Wendell Phillips preach in Parker's place. "I liked him very much," Shaw told his mother. When Fanny Kemble visited Boston in March 1857, Shaw went to hear her read several times. But the steady whirr against slavery tired Shaw, and he lashed out at Kemble, whom Bostonians talked about constantly. He discussed Hinton Rowan Helper's antislavery—and anti-black—polemic, *Impending Crisis* (1857), with a friend who argued that Helper was too poor himself to be able to evaluate slavery fairly and not hold a "grudge against slaveholders."[5]

Even if Shaw could have avoided discussions of slavery at Cambridge, his parents constantly exposed the moral issue in their letters. After Frémont's failure in 1856, a despondent Sarah wrote that she would never live to see "truth & justice prevail in this land." Robert responded that the Republicans would do well in the next election and added, "I can't help hoping that there will be a disunion sometime. . . . Slavery is the only fault in America and we get just as much blame for it as the Southerners, and besides, the disgrace of all their shameful actions." Shaw wanted to rid his nation of slavery but showed little interest in the people who were slaves. The barrage of antislavery voices led him to complain and defend himself to his mother in March 1858: "Because I don't talk and think Slavery all the time, and because I get tired . . . of hearing nothing else, you say I don't feel with you, when I do."[6]

8 NYC Businessman

THE MASSIVE ECONOMIC DEPRESSION called the Panic of 1857 hit both the Shaws and the Curtises hard. Francis Shaw's investments suffered; his income was diminished by nearly half. *Putnam's Magazine* failed, and George William Curtis, a partner, owed huge debts that took him a decade to repay. As Shaw watched these woes, he began to think of alternatives to a business career. He had always enjoyed the outdoors and thought of going into agriculture with a friend, Henry Vezin of Philadelphia, whom he had met in Hanover. Shaw was still considering a "farming project" and "a country life" in the fall of 1858, when his uncles persuaded him to work in their mercantile office in New York. Uncle George Russell in West Roxbury adamantly pushed Shaw "to leave college and not let this opportunity go." Whether Shaw's parents encouraged their brothers to dissuade Shaw from the idea of farming is not known, but they did not stand in the way of his decision. Shaw met with Harvard's president, who assured him that "I could get my degree in a few years after my class graduated." That settled, Shaw withdrew from Harvard. In March 1859 he moved into his old room on Staten Island and entered his uncle's firm, Henry P. Sturgis and Company, in New York City.[1]

Initially, Shaw gloried in his life with his family on Staten Island. He took long rides with his sisters and discussed events with Curtis and his parents. He still entertained ideas of farming with Vezin—in "Virginia, the West, . . . Texas"—but he threw off that fantasy and settled into his duties as a clerk in his uncle's mercantile business and counting room. Shaw expected to pay his dues to the company by working in China sometime in the next three years, but he hoped he would get to spend a summer in England, Germany, and Norway before he went. In July he wrote Vezin, "I expect to do well: I like business very much." By September he rarely got home before eight in the evening, and his tune had changed: "I am a slave now." Shaw did not enjoy the import business and was heartily bored with the long hours and day-to-day drudgery of inventory. He took the early-morning ferry across the East River to Manhattan and the late ferry home after the close of business. He complained to his mother that he had a "hankering after something more 'juicy.'" Shaw wanted to go deer hunting but couldn't spare the time. Longing for carefree adventure and wishing to see Vezin again, he could not break away from work.[2]

Shaw did get a short respite when he visited Buffalo and Toronto after attending the Chicago wedding of his cousin Annie Russell to Alexander Agassiz. A world traveler, Shaw thought Niagara Falls "the greatest sight I ever saw" and wondered about its "roaring" now as it had for thousands of years. He leaned upon his parents for emotional support, and when they left to take his sisters Josephine and Ellen on a cruise to Havana and Nassau in the spring of 1861, Shaw doubted that he had any talent for business and fought depression. He lacked confidence in his managerial abilities and talked with one of the partners, Chandler Robbins, about his concerns. Robbins told him that he just needed more experience and if he stuck with it he would find himself able to succeed at business.[3]

9 New York's Darling Seventh

THE 1860 PRESIDENTIAL RACE excited the nation and the Shaws. George Curtis chaired Staten Island's Republican party and had been to the national nominating convention in Chicago, where he supported the more radical—and Eastern—candidate, William H. Seward of New York. After a westerner named Lincoln won the nomination, Curtis campaigned for the railsplitter. Shaw also voted Republican and watched expectantly for the reaction of the lower South.

The election of Abraham Lincoln was more than Southern white leaders could tolerate. After years of acrimonious compromise over whether the nation would embrace slave or free labor in the expanding western lands, many, North and South, understood that the results of the presidential election would intensify the momentous question of what to do about slavery in a land whose creed emphasized freedom and human liberty. Many people talked of fate and destiny, and agreed with Lincoln's earlier prediction — that, whatever was to come, "a house divided against itself cannot stand." Seward's well-remembered appeals to "Higher Law" and forecast of an "Irrepressible Conflict" guaranteed to many that, whatever was to come, the moral and economic issues of slavery would be decided once and for all.

South Carolina accelerated the movement toward war when it seceded from the Union on December 20, 1860. By the following February, Mississippi, Florida, Alabama, Georgia, Louisiana, and Texas had also voted themselves out of the Union. A fast-moving convention in Montgomery, Alabama, formed the individual republics into the Confederate States of America, and President Jefferson Davis's inaugural address reminded Northerners of "the American idea that governments rest on the consent of the governed." Fourteen days later, Lincoln used his first inaugural to warn Southerners that the Union was "perpetual" and that continuation of the crisis would bring about "the momentous issue of civil war."

As tensions increased, American men and boys raced to join militia groups. In New York City, Robert Gould Shaw enlisted in the unit of high society, the ultra-exclusive Seventh New York National Guard. While he drilled twice weekly in the armory and worked in the counting house of his uncle's mercantile office, Shaw wrote to his family, who were vacationing in the Caribbean, of the "great state of excitement about Fort Sumter. First it was to be evacuated, then re-inforced." On April 5 Shaw told his sister Susanna that he had been a disunionist for about two years, but now wanted "to see the Southern States either brought back by force, or else recognized as independent." He joined other Americans in hoping that Lincoln would "act now with some firmness" and finally confront the issue that had divided the country since its inception. One week later, after South Carolinians fired upon the fort and caused its surrender, Lincoln called for seventy-five thousand men to protect the capitol and help put down the insurrection. As Virginia, Arkansas, North Carolina, and Tennessee joined the Confederacy, Shaw's Seventh Regiment was among the first to respond to Lincoln's most urgent request.[1]

On April 16, the day following Lincoln's call, Marshall Lefferts, commanding the Seventh, notified Governor Edwin Morgan that the regiment stood "ready to march forthwith." Two days later orders came; the regiment would depart the following afternoon at four o'clock, marching down Broadway. With Shaw's father in the Bahamas, Sydney Gay took over the parental role. Gay wrote a note to his wife on April 19: "I saw Theodore Winthrop and Bob [Shaw] off today. The former looked very grave. The latter sent thee this [his boyish photograph] with his love." Even with the short notice, Shaw had just enough time to write letters to his parents, sister Susanna, and George Curtis. He hugged Anna, put on his gray uniform with its starch-white crossbelts, and gladly marched away from his business office to take his place in the excitement of the hour.[2]

The hour would turn into four years of war. But the men of the Seventh—and all but a few Americans—were a long way from realizing that possibility. Shaw thought that "if we can get into Washington, before Virginia begins to make trouble, we shall not have much fighting." This sentiment seemed so certain that the men of the Seventh had agreed to serve only thirty days, even though Lincoln had called for ninety-day volunteers. Shaw entered the war with the naïveté of his generation. Not only would the war be short, but he reassured his mother, and himself, that "there is not much more danger in war than in peace at least for the officers. There are comparatively few men killed." A few days later, on June 10, one of Shaw's childhood friends, Theodore Winthrop, fell dead at the Battle of Big Bethel. Before Shaw met his own fate in July 1863, he endured the pain of losing close Harvard friends at Cedar and South Mountains, Antietam, and Gettysburg. Still, the deaths only made Shaw more dedicated to seeing the war to victory. Increasingly, he was fighting for what he considered his manhood, a manhood wrapped up with the nation's honor.[3]

On April 19, 1861, the "Darling Seventh"—991 men strong— marched down Broadway in the first full flush of war fever. Few New Yorkers stayed at home. Most donned their finest clothes, grabbed top hats, parasols, and bonnets, took their children by the hand, and joined in with a crowd the size of which no one had ever seen before in North America. Those with offices watched from windows as others stood on rooftops five stories above the line of march. Old Glory waved from every building, horses clattered by dragging cannon, and line after line of marching men tried to stay in lockstep as they passed in review. Shaw recalled, "The crowd and enthusiasm were tremendous. The people would hardly let us pass, actually catching hold of our hands and slapping us on the back, yelling and screaming like wild men." Finally, it seemed, the much-awaited war had arrived, and Northern men—and women—were eager to prove themselves up to it. It was a time for bragging, adventure, and adjustment to army life. In a romantic sentiment of nineteenth-century manhood, Shaw ended one of his first military letters hurriedly, with more than a hint of duty and war overtones, "Goodbye, the drum is beating."[4]

Leaving New York, the regiment took a steamer to Philadelphia, then on to Annapolis, Maryland, where it disembarked, spent two days at the U.S. Naval Academy, and navigated down a road "full of Secessionists," before becoming the first unit to reach the capital after Lincoln's call for volunteers. Forever afterward the Seventh would proclaim itself "the regiment that saved the capital!" The unit had reacted like minutemen, and Shaw excitedly joined men from all over the Union who gathered "ready to fight for the country, as the old fellows did in the Revolution." The regimental band regularly played sentimental ballads to keep the men entertained and nationalistic. Shaw was warmed by the resurgent note of patriotism whenever "we hear the national airs, and look at the stars and stripes, with new emotions in an enemy's country."[5]

Believing in the widely held notion that a "Slave Power" conspiracy had ruled the nation for much too long, Shaw exulted that it was great to be in Washington "bullying the Southerners." This pampered son and regiment had a great deal of fun parading around for civilians, being quartered in the House of Representatives while their engineer corps readied a tented encampment outside the city center, and touring the capital. It was not exactly like war, yet. Shaw had many close friends and cousins with him in what must have seemed more like a club outing than preparation for battle.[6]

On his second day in Washington, Shaw got his first close look at the new commander-in-chief when the regiment was sworn in as "thirty-day men." Playing off preelection jokes that the president was the ugliest man in America—and a hick too—Shaw immediately wrote his mother: "'Old Abe' . . . took off his hat in the most awkward way, putting it on again with his hand on the back part of the rim, country fashion. A boy came by with a pail of water for us, and the President took a great swig from it as it passed. I couldn't help thinking of the immense responsibility he has on his shoulders, as he stood there laughing and talking. I have seen many uglier men."[7]

A few days later, Shaw and Private Rufus King, son of the president of Columbia College, called at the White House and were treated to a handshake and a "five minute conversation" with the president in the Oval Office. As he had done with thousands, Lincoln charmed Shaw by the "very striking face" and gentle manner. Shaw was surprised that he talked without the hint of "Western slang or twang in him." That same afternoon, Shaw met Secretary of State William Seward, whom he judged "a very kind old gentleman, but not so cordial as Mr. Lincoln & not nearly so firm & decided." At any rate, the young Shaw had an ever-expanding circle of prominent acquaintances in the small nineteenth-century world of the elite.[8]

Losing their sleeping accommodations in Congress, the Seventh moved into tents two miles east of the White House. In the most crowded bedroom of his life, Shaw slept with five other men in a tent he named "Virtue's Bower." He drilled daily, spent long hours predicting what might happen and when, wrote home, and drifted through an easy time of service. The war certainly did not end during the thirty-day enlistment period of the Seventh New York. Private Shaw decided that there was as much of a reason to stay in as there had been to come out in the first place.[9]

10 Officer Rank and Loyalty

WHILE THE SEVENTH DISBANDED and many of its members returned to civilian life, Shaw remained a soldier. Using the power of his family name, he quickly gained an officer's commission in the newly approved Second Massachusetts Infantry. One of the first three-year regiments organized during the Civil War, the Second Massachusetts had a pick of officers and men and had no trouble filling its ranks with educated soldiers. The new regiment formed and trained at Camp Andrew—named for the state's governor, John A. Andrew—at West Roxbury, site of the Brook Farm experiment. That in itself added to the mystique—and reality—of Brahmin power, as the force in arms muscled past the intellectual power of transcendentalism. For Shaw, being back "home" seemed "very odd" and brought back wonderful memories of childhood innocence in a simpler time.[1]

During his twenty months in the Brahmin regiment, Shaw learned about the love that grows from depending on others for life. Parents, sisters, cousins, and childhood and college friends were held dear, but that was not the same affection as that which a soldier reveals to a comrade on the field of battle, around the campfires of an army, or in the tents of a regiment. With fear, hate, and love so near each other that one easily turned into another, a soldier felt all three at once. Afraid to be injured or killed or called a coward, a man could take another's life and convince himself that he hated him, all the while admiring him, knowing that he felt and acted the same way. When the battles ended, friends frantically searched one for the other, but they also did what could be done for those they had just been trying to kill. Killing one moment, trying to save the next, hating then consoling the enemy in acts of tremendous violence interspersed with tender mercies, Shaw felt these emotions, and he brought them to bear on his fellow officers. He knew that his friends in the Second were dearer to him than any he had made before. He depended on them, and they on him, for life and honor. They shared experiences that no one who had not been with them could imagine. And even if someone could imagine, Shaw and his comrades knew that only they really understood how they felt for each other because of the mingling of three very different yet similar emotions into an inseparable unity in a time of great stress.

Signing up for three years and commissioned a second lieutenant, Shaw found the life of an officer much different from that of a common soldier. Of course the pay differed. Privates got $13.00 a month, plus a $3.50 clothing allowance. Second Lieutenant Shaw received $150.00, "part of two months pay." Shaw noted other benefits: "We have cots to sleep on, much better fare, and servants in abundance from among the men." Whenever the situation allowed, Shaw arranged to live and board in private homes near the regimental campground. He concluded that this was "a Christian and reasonable" approach, in contrast to "the rest [who] dine in the woods." When outside boarding proved unobtainable, Shaw joined other officers in meals provided by a steward or by "servants" assigned from the ranks. After lunch—in the early days of the war—he enjoyed "the time to lie round, & smoke, read or sleep" before camp duties ended with supper. In the evenings he managed "to have a great deal of fun in one way and another."[2]

Shaw wanted promotion and got it, advancing to a captaincy; but those promotions were based more on the deaths of senior officers than on Shaw's abilities. He learned to be a good officer who carried out orders, but he became neither a spectacular tactical nor strategic commander. When those who knew him spoke of him, they emphasized his loyalty, gentleness, and obedience, not his military acumen. As the war lengthened, Shaw had chances to advance by changing regiments or accepting staff positions with general officers. He told himself he wanted a better position, often thought about getting a commission in the regular army, and watched for opportunities. During the first year of the war, Shaw would have transferred to obtain a higher commission. But after the Second lost men in battles and feelings of loyalty settled around him and his friends, only something extraordinary could pry him away from the regiment.[3]

11 John Brown and a Disciplined Army

FOR MANY AMERICANS of Shaw's era and for some later historians, the Civil War started not in Charleston Harbor on April 12, 1861, but in an unlikely Virginia river town on October 16, 1859. At Harper's Ferry, remarkable only because of the U.S. arsenal located there, the radical abolitionist John Brown led an "army" of twenty-one liberators in a plan to seize the arsenal and distribute the weapons to black Virginians. According to God's plan as revealed to Brown, this slave army would roar through the South killing slaveholders, freeing humans from bondage, and growing larger with new recruits from the plantations. Brown envisioned an atonement for the nation's sins as Jehovah used him, a new Joshua, to slay the sinners and free the innocent.

Shaw's parents and circle of friends had fervently supported Brown. The Unitarian leader Theodore Parker christened Brown "a saint," Lydia Maria Child's open letters to Brown and Governor Henry Wise of Virginia escalated the verbal war, and Ralph Waldo Emerson claimed that Brown made "the gallows as glorious as the cross." Thus, in 1861 and again in 1862, when the Second Massachusetts Infantry occupied Harper's Ferry, Lieutenant Shaw got an inside look at the town forever heroized by the man called by Herman Melville "the Meteor of the War."[1]

Shaw took up quarters in the law office of Andrew Hunter, the attorney who had prosecuted Brown. Shaw's unstoppable—if very human—rifling of Hunter's files brought forth "piles of letters and papers" from Lydia Child, former President Buchanan, and others, "some interceding for Brown, and some hoping and praying that he would be executed without delay." Sending home a souvenir paper written by one of Brown's men, Shaw rationalized, "I don't think there is anything wrong with in it. . . . and we are not to blame for making good our opportunities to examine the papers of such a traitor as he is."[2]

In 1861 Lieutenant Shaw reflected approvingly on the deeds of the Meteor even while he challenged Brown's military skills. He visited the engine house where Brown made his last stand and ultimately surrendered to Colonel Robert E. Lee of the U.S. Army. Shaw thought it "the worst place he could have chosen to defend . . . for when the doors are shut, it is like a brick box." The Second Massachusetts used it as the guardhouse. Shaw also took a short horseback ride over to Charlestown, where he toured the jail cell that confined Brown until he swung from the gallows in an open field not far up the hill. Obviously inspired by what he saw and still quartered near Harper's Ferry, Shaw hoped that the government would soon "call on all the blacks in the country to come and enlist in our army!" Not only would they make excellent spies, but they "would probably make a fine army after a little drill."[3]

While Shaw reckoned with the ghost of John Brown and the reasons Northern soldiers marched upon Southern soils, the first major battle of the war was being fought at Manassas Junction, on the banks of a stream called Bull Run. The Southern victory sent panic throughout the North and brought either the realization that the conflict would be a long one or the fear that the South was nearing independence. Shaw ruminated openly: "I sincerely hope the war will not finish without a good, fair battle, as we should never hear the end of Bull Run." Fighting not against slavery or even for union, Shaw fought solely, at first, for honor and bragging rights.[4]

Following the loss at First Bull Run, Northern armies in the

Eastern Theater put more effort into training and discipline than into searching out and fighting Southern armies. The new commander of the Army of the Potomac, General George B. McClellan, worked hard to transform raw recruits into competent soldiers. Lieutenant Shaw admired "Little Mac's" abilities as "doing wonders . . . for all the regiments have improved very much in respect of discipline" and are "never troubled as formerly by stragglers." He was decidedly against the practice of having officers selected by the men, believing that discipline could not be maintained when officers "owe their places" to election.[5]

For the first time in his life, Shaw had to deal with men of all classes. Growing up in the world of the educated and rich at Brook Farm, Fordham, Neuchâtel, Hanover, Harvard, and in the business circles of New York City, Shaw had few dealings with the less fortunate. But as an officer he could no longer avoid them. He had always enjoyed the power of money, and now he held the power of rank.

Feeling that strict adherence to rules and good conduct made for more effective armies, Shaw supported the common practice of "gagging and tying [offenders] to trees whenever they were unruly." He ridiculed officers who could not keep their men in line, and he highly respected those who strictly followed regulations made for regular army soldiers. The severity of discipline and the distance between officers and men in the Second Massachusetts was often a subject of ridicule by other volunteer units and by men writing their hometown papers about overbearing officers. But Shaw scoffed at such criticism from enlisted men and believed that civilians were in no place to understand an officer's duty.[6]

To Shaw, the Second was the army's best regiment because of its adherence to order. "A soldier is not a soldier," he insisted, without the wonder of discipline. Shaw vented his deepest criticism on the Irish—whom he distinguished from "Americans"—consistently berating their abilities as soldiers. Undoubtedly these feelings had grown as he watched the Irish buttressing the Democratic party against the abolitionists. Here again, Shaw was unforgiving.[7]

In keeping with his "us against them" mind-set, Shaw laughed at or scorned many of the Southerners he met, often ridiculing them as stupid. The especially ignorant ones were always those who challenged the North's supremacy or castigated Northern troops. One girl in Frederick, Maryland, told Shaw: "I like a nigger better than a Massachusetts soldier." In Edinburg, Virginia, Shaw labeled the inhabitants "a nasty, dirty, ignorant race." Another time, Shaw told his mother about a "screaming, swearing, bawling, & blubbering" family whose mother was "not ladylike." He said that the common people did not even know what the war was about.[8]

12 Camp Life in Virginia

LIEUTENANT SHAW ADAPTED quickly to the roving camp life of armies in the field. He enjoyed sights he had never seen and was quite the tourist in letters telling of scenery, weather, and oddities in a "wish you were here" tone. He enjoyed rummaging through the private letters and personal property of Southerners, particularly women, in homes he boarded in or broke into. He drank wine and smoked cigars with his new civilian companions and his "old" military friends. After the years in the scholarly and business worlds, where he felt ill cast, Shaw had returned, in many ways, to the merrymaking of his Hanover years. One year after he marched off to war, he exulted in his good fortune: "What a blessing that we happened to be born in this century and country!"[1]

Shaw fell into the measured pace of camp life and formed new friendships while maintaining old friends in the regiment. He found himself better suited to soldiering than to office work and wrote happily: "Isn't it a strange sort of life for us to be living who never expected to be anything but merchants & lawyers three months ago?" A little later he continued, "What a difference between October 1860 and October 1861 in America—and where will we all be next year at this time?" Never religious, he attended Sunday sermons—sometimes with as many as ten thousand soldiers and ten preachers engaged at once. He met Abner Doubleday, the inventor of baseball, even though he never played the game himself in camp. In his spare time, which was abundant, Shaw liked to read. He also kept up a heavy letter-writing schedule, informing family and friends of his activities in and reflections of army life. In return, he got so many letters that he found it "almost impossible to answer them all."[2]

While Shaw enjoyed himself, his parents vacationed in fashionable northern watering holes and sporadically, particularly when the Second took up winter quarters, visited their son in camp. They provided comfort in the form of photographs, books, vegetables, cigars, and material accoutrements or finer uniforms not provided by the U.S. Army or the state of Massachusetts. Although he lived mostly in a world of men, Shaw sought any opportunity for companionship with women. For the most part, female company came from visitors to camp, but sometimes, when near a town or house with Union sympathizers, the officers were invited to dine or to attend grand balls. In the prime of young manhood, Shaw remarked often about his feelings when encountering "real ladies with petticoats about." At a night-long ball in Maryland, Shaw joined three hundred other men and a hundred women. "I enjoyed myself very much though and danced nearly all the time. . . . Frederick seems to be full of pretty and nice girls, and the officers who live in town are having a very gay time."[3]

Life in camp was as dangerous as participation in battle. While Shaw hoped to prove himself under arms, he fought and won a

contest that for many soldiers proved more fatal than bullets—
dysentery. But, unlike most other soldiers who suffered the sickness in field hospitals, Shaw set himself up in a room in a house
with a private nurse. Beyond that suffering, he happily lived "a
regular old jog trot camp life" while he waited for battle. Shaw
conceded a lengthy war, knowing "we shall have much more soldiering to do than we expected when we started."[4]

13 What War Really Is: Antietam

WINTER MELTED into spring in 1862, and amid the renewal of
nature and rebirth of Easter, American armies turned the season
into a time of death and burial. Federal troops made major ad-
vances. In the west a Yankee nova exploded as Ulysses S. Grant
won victories at Shiloh and Forts Donelson and Henry. In the east
McClellan launched his peninsular campaign against Richmond.
Off Hampton Roads, two ironclads, the *Monitor* and the *Merri-
mack*, dueled to a draw.

After a year of campaigning, Lieutenant Shaw had neither fired
his pistol nor raised his sword against the enemy. Adept at drill, he
still questioned his ability to fight and ached for the time when
he could prove his valor. Friends in other regiments had been
tested in several fights, some had died, and more than a few—like
Oliver Wendell Holmes, Jr.—had received honorable wounds;
Shaw wanted the same chance.

While he took in the beauty of springtime in Virginia, he
marched and countermarched between Winchester, Strasburg, and
New Market as the army of General Nathaniel Banks chased after Stonewall Jackson—the South's new star. Jackson outmarched
and outdodged three Federal armies playing tag with them and
sometimes, unexpectedly, stopping to fight his pursuers. Shaw en-

dured wearying marches and hot weather hunting for the phantom Jackson. He described a nineteen-hour struggle through a hard rain—with muddy roads and swollen streams—until he fell bone-tired into a tent bivouac under the bombarding drips of water falling from the trees above. He did manage some pleasures during the campaign, even seeing Belle Boyd with friends at Front Royal. Shaw adamantly—and incorrectly—ridiculed newspaper accounts that the nineteen-year-old beauty was a spy for Stonewall Jackson. Of course his genteel upbringing placing women in different spheres, and his soldier's uniform, evoking a conquistador masculinity, prevented him from realizing the obvious. Boyd—and Jackson—benefited from the chauvinism.[1]

On March 24, 1862, Shaw visited a field hospital and wrote to his mother as if he had been just initiated into the war. There were "about 20 dead men laid out, with the capes of their overcoats folded over their faces." When Shaw pulled back the capes, checking to see if any of his "college-acquaintances" had fallen, he was surprised "to see the dead & wounded Ohio men & Virginians lying there side by side." The reality of a civil war had finally forced itself onto Shaw, and he realized that such things "are horrible to see or to think of—but such scenes show us, more than anything else, what war really is." Then, reflecting a common trait in the human spirit, he righted himself, manfully, and told his mother: "It is astonishing though, how soon one gets accustomed to terrible sights. The second time I went to the Hospital I found myself looking about, as if I had lived all my life among dead & wounded men."[2]

Two months later, in the valley of the Shenandoah River, suddenly and for the next two days, Shaw's regiment careened into the Stonewall. During the battles at Front Royal and Winchester, the Second Massachusetts got its first taste of combat. Citing the confusion of defeat and retreat, Shaw disliked seeing "our men tumbling over" but thought it "not so horrid a sight as the battle-field

& the wounded after the excitement is over." In a hurry to escape Jackson's onslaught, the regiment marched thirty-four miles one day and nearly twenty-six the next. Even so, Shaw deemed it "a perfect wonder that the army got away safely."[3]

He was even more lucky not to have been killed when a minié ball passed through his clothes and struck directly into the pocket-watch hanging from his vest. Shaw remembered only "a violent blow and a burning sensation in my side." At Front Royal the attack came so unexpectedly as to catch the untried officer without his weapons, his revolver and sword packed away neatly in his luggage. Borrowing a "toy-sword" from a drummer boy, Shaw managed to direct his company through the hard fighting, losing nine men killed and wounded of the fifty engaged under his command. A sergeant later complimented him for showing "a great deal of courage and coolness" under fire. That kind of praise—and the fact that he was alive with a small wound—confirmed that he had passed the test of battle. He had also passed the test of being an officer, at least in the eyes of the enlisted men who ridiculed "college boys" as political appointees who might not fight like men.[4]

With Union armies unable to corner Jackson along the Shenandoah—and being defeated when they did—and with McClellan and Lincoln bickering publicly over the failure of the campaign to take Richmond, Shaw and the Northern public uneasily watched the changing fortunes of war. There was a long pause in the fighting along the eastern front as both sides jockeyed for position. Shaw thought things "at a stand-still . . . [perhaps] a lull before the storm."[5]

Lincoln called for another three hundred thousand men, making a total of one million Northerners put into service since the war began. In times of inaction, soldiers universally complain more about their leaders than during periods of high activity. Shaw thought the strategic problems of the army were due to the "republican form of government [that] never managed the country with a firm hand." He even suggested that a dictator might be the most acceptable solution for a while. And, in the usual way that soldiers begin to trust other soldiers and resent civilians who have never been under arms, he sighed, "We may finish the war, but it will certainly be with a much greater loss of time, life, and money than if we had had some men, any man almost, with a few common-sense military ideas, to manage matters, without being meddled with and badgered by a lot of men who show the greatest ignorance about the commonest things."[6]

The lull passed and the storm came surging furiously across the land in a wave of blood still unsurpassed on North American soil. The Second Massachusetts was involved in a frightful bloodletting at Cedar Mountain on August 9. Stationed in a wheatfield and caught in a crossfire, the regiment was cut to pieces. In the aftermath of the fighting, Captain Shaw wrote home in a letter similar to the type received almost daily by families during the war: "We had a hard fight yesterday . . . the Second Massachusetts [suffered] more than the rest. Captains Cary, Williams, Abbott, and Goodwin, and Lieutenant Perkins were killed. Major Savage wounded and taken [prisoner]; Lieutenants Robeson, Oakey, Browning, and Grafton wounded, and sent to Alexandria. Captains Russell and Quincy, and Lieutenant Miller, prisoners. Surgeon Leland also wounded."[7]

In thirty minutes of fighting, the Second Massachusetts had 16 of its 23 officers killed or wounded, 49 enlisted men killed, 99 wounded, and 14 captured or missing. These numbers reflect part of the 466 total casualties in Gordon's 1,500-man Brigade during the hellish half-hour firefight with Stonewall Jackson. Total losses on both sides were 3,821 men. Stunned by the news of so many friends dead and of family member Harry Russell made a prisoner, Shaw's family cried happily and prayed fervently when they read, "I can't conceive how I could have got through without a scratch." They also read Shaw's praise of manliness among his friends, some of whom were "quite ill." Shaw praised their honorable deaths: "It was splendid to see those sick fellows walk straight up into the shower of bullets, as if it were so much rain."[8]

Just over a month later, the storm intensified on one terrible Wednesday along Antietam Creek, Maryland, when Lee's Army of Northern Virginia pounded suicidally at McClellan's confused, but competent, Army of the Potomac. When the fighting ended, six thousand men lay dead or dying, and seventeen thousand more suffered wounds. Shaw's Second fought its way back and forth across a cornfield, alternately taking and giving up possession to the Confederates. Shaw was thrilled by it all: by a marching maneuver that was "the prettiest thing we have ever done"; by "such a mass of dead and wounded men . . . I never saw before"; by what he considered "the greatest fight of the war." He experienced the ancient script written by men in war, a rising of the blood that simultaneously electrified and frightened him: "I never felt, before, the excitement which makes a man want to rush into the fight, but I did that day. . . . It seems almost as if nothing could justify a battle like that of the 17th, and the horrors inseparable from it."[9]

Captain Shaw lived through the Battle of Antietam even while receiving his second wound. This time, unlike the minié ball that smashed violently into his watch at Front Royal, the Antietam projectile had already lost its killing velocity before arching into his neck and bouncing away. Only bruised, he was one of the lucky ones. In the forty days from the Cedar Mountain wheatfield on August 9 to the Antietam cornfield on September 17, Shaw watched his friends, fellow officers, and men fall around him— 243 casualties, 80 men killed.[10]

The young man who marched off to war hoping for a chance to fight perhaps got more than he wanted. Certainly he came to see the folly in his pronouncement the previous summer that there was "not much more danger in war than in peace." Like others, he became accustomed to a surreal, but all too horrible, existence. In the aftermath of Antietam, Shaw elegantly described his growing complacency with war scenes, "At last, night came on, and, with the exception of an occasional shot from the outposts, all was quiet. The crickets chirped, and the frogs croaked, just as if nothing unusual had happened all day long, and presently the stars came out bright, and we lay down among the dead, and slept soundly until daylight. There were twenty dead bodies within a rod of me." [11]

Shaw had always wanted to be among those who had "seen the elephant"—a soldier's phrase for battle. After Cedar Mountain and Antietam, he joined them. Saddened by deaths, Shaw never lost his enthusiasm for the fight, not even when he was assigned as the officer for the dead. In that job Shaw supervised the removal of bodies—of which many had been close friends or colleagues—from the field and packed them in charcoal, sending them off to be placed into metal coffins for shipment northward. He conceived it "a fearful thing" to see two hundred men dead who had been alive moments before; but in his next sentence, Shaw hoped to "live long enough to see [Rebels] running before us hacked to little pieces." Revenge was a prominent part of the cult of masculinity, and Shaw was not immune to its power to keep men in the army and to keep them fighting for one another.[12]

In the aftermath of Antietam, McClellan failed to press Lee's weakened army. In fact, McClellan resisted moving the Army of the Potomac even after Lincoln visited camp and lived in a tent beside him. When he finally acted, on October 26, it was too late. After midterm congressional elections indicated public dissatisfaction with the war, Lincoln—frustrated with the slowness of McClellan—ended the general's career by replacing him with Ambrose Burnside on November 5. Eleven weeks later, after Burnside's reckless assault at Fredericksburg and the infamous "mud march," Lincoln placed Joseph Hooker in his stead. The North's showcase army had changed commanders three times in three months.

Physically depleted, Captain Shaw and the Second Massachusetts did not participate in the fight at Fredericksburg but stayed in quarters at Sharpsburg, Maryland, and Fairfax Station, Virginia. Trying to make sense of what had happened, Shaw vascillated between ideas of a long struggle and a contest shortened by the "Peace Party." Lincoln's sacking of McClellan, whom Shaw admired above all other officers, brought on a lot of self-reflection. And another presidential action loomed prominently in Captain Shaw's eyes. Five days after the slaughter at Antietam, Lincoln announced, preliminarily, that as of January 1 next, all slaves held in areas "in rebellion against the United States, shall be then, thenceforward, and forever free."

 Annie Haggerty

HOLIDAYS ARE DIFFICULT and joyous celebrations for most of us. Family and friends gather round, there is time for eating and laughing, old arguments or rivalries surface, stories are told and retold, and rituals link Christian Americans to Puritan Massachusetts and Bethlehem's promise. In 1862 the season filled with melancholy in a nation at war with itself. Captain Shaw was in winter camp with his regiment, recovering still from the Antietam fight and contemplating the future.

Camped "close by the great battle-field" and unable to forget the past, Shaw often retraced the events that took place there. Alone, or together with a friend or two, Shaw rode over the undulating, rock-filled fields stretched out below the Dunkard Church, where the bulk of the slaughter took place. He located places where his comrades had fallen and retold stories of the fight. It took only a little imagination to reconstruct the horror as the decaying carcasses of dead horses littered the four-mile stretch of field toward Antietam bridge. In one spot Shaw counted sixteen horses melting together in one heap—the entire team of one Union battery. Every tree held the scars or lead of minié balls, half the houses showed damage from artillery rounds, and, as Shaw succinctly stated, "the place is full of graves." Here and there, straight rows of dead soldiers—as many as forty in a line—lay silently in massive, common, two-month-old gravesites that spoke loudly of brave and tragic sacrifice. And the dead rested uneasily; teams of diggers pulled the known from single graves as families reclaimed bodies of their loved ones for a bitter homecoming and reinterment in Northern soil.[1]

Just a year had passed since an uninitiated, battleless Shaw had lived through a similar holiday period. That time the regiment "had enjoyed itself very much." There was optimism at the church service, and afterward nine hundred men dined on ninety-four turkeys, seventy-six geese, seventy-three chickens, and "twelve hundred pounds of plum pudding." The band played and the men danced. Officers ate together in a mess tent "gorgeously lighted with candles, bayonets serving for candlesticks, and the dinner was excellent." Christmas parties in nearby Frederick, Maryland, had offered female companionship.[2]

November and December 1862 put up a different picture. Winter exceeded itself with the most bitter cold anyone could remember, as snow and rain fought each other for dominance. At Thanksgiving dinner, Shaw "missed from the table so many faces which were there last year at this time." Thanking God for his many blessings proved to be "a very quiet affair" because of those who were not there: "seven officers killed . . . [and] a good many at home wounded and ill." Christmas brought even more sorrow for missing comrades, as Burnside's futile assault against Marye's Heights at Fredericksburg on December 13 cost 12,653 casualties of the 121,000 Union troops dashing headlong into Robert E. Lee.[3]

Confused by the course of recent events, Shaw had inklings of joining the cavalry, but his loyalty to his unit blocked that option. News of the battle deaths of his first cousin Theodore Parkman, his Harvard classmate Arthur Dehon, and George Curtis's brother Joe made him worry over his own future even while it steeled him to continue the fight for the sacred memory of his fallen friends. Shaw believed "that the officers that have been killed were the very best we had, both as comrades and as military men," and he pledged retribution and honor. "I had rather stay here all my life," he said, "than give up to the South."[4]

While experiencing the love-hate relationship of the battlefield, where casualties brought an ever-changing society and where insecurity of life itself dominated everyday affairs, Shaw sought stability by writing letters home. He did what men typically do in wartime—and in peacetime too, of course—he sought security and an ensured future by seeking and loving a woman. In times of war, particularly, home and women define life when foreign soils and men mean death. Letters from home have always helped keep men at war. Any time Shaw went a day or week without receiving mail, his spirits flagged a bit, and he often implored his sisters or his girlfriend, Annie, to "write to me often, . . . for I need a word occasionally from those whom I love, to keep up my courage."[5]

He met Annie Haggerty in the months before the war, when his sister Susanna arranged a small party for the opera. He was taken by the younger woman, who almost matched him in height, color of eyes and hair, but whose oval face and wavy hair—even if most of it was held tightly under a knitted hairpiece—entranced him. Then and there, on what must have in 1862 seemed such a long-ago night, Shaw decided to one day take her as "my young woman." Socially acceptable as a rich man's bride, Annie came from a wealthy family with a summer house in the Berkshire Mountains at Lenox, Massachusetts. Her father, Ogden Haggerty, inherited and made a fortune in an auction and commission house, Haggerty and Company, in New York City. The Haggertys knew the Shaws through business contacts and because Sarah often visited Lenox to escape the heat of Boston and to visit friends in the abolitionist movement.[6]

Shaw saw Annie only a few times, but army life increased his longing for her. As early as August 1861, he asked Susanna to send him a picture of Annie but adolescently implored, "I don't want you to get it from her." Giving portraits as favors was fashionable during the *carte de visite* fad of the time, and Shaw's mother sent Annie's mother four pictures of him in his uniform. Shaw started writing to Annie, and when she showed interest by writing back, he arranged to see her whenever he could get a chance to visit Staten Island or Lenox. Their relationship grew stronger with the anticipation of the touching, reading, and smelling of words inscribed on stationery and delivered by the post office.[7]

Sometime shortly after Antietam, he proposed marriage and waited through two suspenseful weeks for a response. When it came, he sulked that "she didn't say 'Yes' outright, but . . . it will come all right in the end." His rash assumption that her "maybe" meant "yes" caused him a few weeks of turmoil as he waited for a more definitive answer. But their correspondence served to move them steadily toward the altar. To take brides, men have to sever the looser or tighter ties with their mothers. Shaw took this step fairly late in life. By November 23, 1862, he was able to make the ultimate commitment to Annie by confiding, "I felt wicked when I told you I wanted to see you even more than Mother; for I have always loved her more than any one else in the world. . . . But it was true, nevertheless, like every-thing I have written to you, and a great deal more besides." But leaving little to chance and with the thought of marriage "mak[ing] me feel very happy," Shaw enlisted his mother in the cause of winning Annie, imploring her to "have a talk with [Annie] about it."[8]

Sarah Shaw thought her son "bold" but thrilled Robert with her approval, saying he "shall be a fortunate fellow to get her." Shaw's letters to Annie responded to her worry that he might stay in the army when the war ended. He allayed her fears, while assuring her of his sense of duty and honor: "I once thought of doing so, but have not for a good while. . . . It must be a good-for-nothing sort of life in time of peace. . . . but if the war goes on, there will be just as much reason for my doing my share in it as there was for coming out in the beginning." He wanted her to call him Robert or Rob instead of Bob. They exchanged many letters when she got upset because he had been indiscreet in telling his mother that she would marry him when she felt she hadn't agreed finally to do so. Apologizing in "such a melancholy and humble vein," he persuaded her to forgave him. But even after Annie finally yielded to his persistence, the couple kept the engagement a secret from everyone but their parents and Susanna until February.[9]

While Shaw dreamed about Annie, he continued with the daily life of winter camp. With his constant companion and cousin, Harry Russell, he shared a nine-by-nine-foot log house with a tent roof and an open brick fireplace. Sometimes it was difficult to keep warm, even wrapped up in the buffalo robe blankets sent by his father. Additionally, "washing is a terrible ordeal," ink froze during writing, and he found it hard "'to come up to scratch' every morning." Then, suddenly, headquarters granted him a ten-day furlough, which he divided between Annie in Lenox and his family on Staten Island. During that time Annie sealed her commitment to Robert, even though he still worried over it once he returned to his regiment in Virginia. In any off moment he found himself gazing at the vignette of Annie he carried always in his pocket. A short week after leaving Lenox, he anxiously wrote, "I have thought a great deal of you—indeed almost all the time since I left Lenox—and of my visit to you, especially the last part of it. O, dear! you don't know how much I should like to see you again!" Two weeks later he still ached for her, "I want to see you *horribly* (that is the only word I can think of for it)." He was soon to get his wish: the opportunity to join her came as suddenly as a meteor from heaven.[10]

15 Emancipation Proclamation

SHAW ONLY OCCASIONALLY spoke of the "peculiar institution," and his letters rarely reveal his thoughts about it. He did know that the war began over the issue of human bondage, and, while mentioning the "crime of slavery," he offered little else. In 1861 he had informed his mother that the slaves around John Brown's prison in Charlestown, Virginia, seemed "well cared for but they are evidently glad to see us." His descriptions of "the delighted darkies" and his regular use of the term "nigger" revealed his prejudices. Yet, while most Union officers ignored the preliminary Emancipation Proclamation in their letters home, Shaw took notice of it. He thought it was of little value militarily and, because of an expected Confederate response, believed "the evil will overbalance the good for the *present*." Shaw quickly added that after the war ended, "after we have subdued them [the Confederates], it will be a great thing." As for the wrong of slavery, Shaw wrote that it belonged "entirely to another people." He positively placed himself on the side that was freeing the slaves, but his attitude was based more on honor than on egalitarianism. He was an early supporter of the use of blacks as soldiers. Believing that white soldiers would at first complain but then get used to the idea of having blacks in the ranks, Shaw thought blacks would "make a fine army after a little drill, and could certainly be kept under better discipline than our independent Yankees." [1]

From the beginning of the war, some few voices consistently called for the inclusion of blacks in the military. The most persistent urging came from Frederick Douglass. He determined that military service for blacks was a revolutionary move that should herald both freedom for the slaves and citizenship rights for all African Americans. In 1861—just three weeks after Lincoln's initial call for troops—Douglass suggested, "Let the slaves and free colored people be called into service, and formed into a liberating army, to march into the South and raise the banner of emancipation among the slaves." In the same address Douglass sounded much like an Old Testament prophet, warning and scolding, "Until the nation shall repent of this weakness and folly, until they shall make the cause of their country the cause of freedom, until they shall strike down slavery, the source and center of this gigantic rebellion, they don't deserve the support of a single sable arm." As early as August 30, 1861, and well ahead of his compatriots, Major General John Frémont, in Missouri, had freed the slaves; Lincoln quickly vetoed that action. Next, Major General David Hunter's emancipation order of May 9, 1862, declared that "slavery and martial law in a free country are altogether incompatible," and all former slaves in his command, the Department of the South, "are therefore declared forever free." After hearing of Hunter's decree, an obviously pleased Francis Shaw wrote to Garrison, "Has not the President used a very sharp knife, in Genl Hunter's hands, to cut the knot." Three days later, Shaw felt betrayed when Lincoln revoked Hunter's proclamation. [2]

Lincoln was a savvy politician. He continued to worry about what northern slaveholding whites and their allies would do if he complied with the calls for emancipation from Douglass, Frémont, Hunter, and thousands of slaves. Finally, in late 1862, with the war going badly, recruitment falling off, casualties mounting, and the threat of aid to the Confederacy from England or France in the air, Lincoln acted. With the victory at Antietam, he issued the preliminary Emancipation Proclamation as notice of what was to come if the South did not lay down its arms. Additionally, this preliminary proclamation gave him time to judge Northern reaction and for the voting populace to get used to the idea. Many still held that this was a white man's war. Lincoln received letters of support from abolitionist groups and from lone voices who agreed in the need for black enlistment. From Massachusetts came a letter from the Republican electors of 1860 telling Lincoln they had "happily certified" his election two years ago and now "congratulate you upon your having begun the greatest act in American history, the emancipation" of the slaves. They ended the letter with a call "to let blacks fight for us."[3]

Republicans knew that Lincoln had stepped onto precarious political ground. Ten days before the Emancipation Proclamation would take effect, Massachusetts Congressman Charles Sedgwick wrote to John Forbes, a high-powered industrialist, Lincoln advisor, and Shaw's cousin: "Be ready to shout Hallelujah on the morning of 1st January, and let the President know that he is to have sympathy and support. By all means, put him up to practical measures to make it a success. Tell him the world will pardon his crimes, and his stories even, if he only makes the proclamation a success, and that if he fails he will be gibbeted in history as a great, long-legged, awkward, country pettifogger, without brains or backbone." Lincoln did have backbone and historical savvy.[4]

During the early months of 1863, Lincoln and Congress acted to secure men for the Union armies. On March 3 Congress passed the Enrollment Act, which authorized a draft of all men of ages twenty to forty-five to serve a three-year enlistment. That conscription act caused riots in Northern cities and was nearly as unpopular as the North's other new focus for soldier procurement.

On January 1 the Emancipation Proclamation freed the slaves, and in late January Lincoln authorized Secretary of War Edwin M. Stanton to enlist black men into volunteer regiments. Many people who supported the war for union lashed out at Lincoln for changing the goal of the war to one for freedom of the slaves. The idea of black men in uniforms with guns frightened some Northerners and most Southerners. Many white soldiers loathed the idea of serving with black soldiers. Nevertheless, Lincoln persisted; after all, with the war going badly, he had nothing to lose and everything to gain by more manpower. Once he announced the Emancipation Proclamation and authorized the raising of black regiments, the war turned. Moral suasion had failed to free the slaves; now the sons of slaves would free themselves and guarantee a Union victory.

Before the war ended, 178,975 African Americans, one-twelfth of all the soldiers for the Union, joined the armed forces of the North. They fought in 145 infantry regiments, 7 cavalry groups, 13 artillery units, and 1 engineering battalion. At least 60 of these 166 units fought on the battlefield; the others performed garrison duty. Black sailors had been enlisted since the war began and by war's end made up one-fourth of all seamen. Black men who had been born free joined with black men who had run away from slavery or had been freed by Union armies to strike a blow for the destruction of slavery. The most amazing single statistic is that approximately 34,000 of 46,150 (74%) free Northern blacks of military age, 18 to 45, fought for their country, fought for themselves. Overall, counting Southern freedmen, nearly 37,000 black soldiers died from wounds or disease.[5]

16 Soldiers of African Descent

AMONG THE REGIMENTS raised in the North, the Fifty-fourth Massachusetts Infantry led the way. Governor Andrew, who strongly advocated using blacks in the military, had helped form and lead the Free Soil and Republican parties in Massachusetts. He was elected governor in 1860 and served five one-year terms beginning on January 2, 1861. An abolitionist, Andrew wanted to prove that black men would fight—which would in turn prove that they were men and thus entitled to be free citizens. A politician, he hoped that black enlistment would take the pressure off his state to meet its enlistment quotas. If Lincoln failed to enlist blacks in the war, Andrew would have to fill quotas with factory workers, a thought loathed by business interests in this most industrialized state in the Union. Businessmen in Massachusetts— and elsewhere—supported the Emancipation Proclamation out of economic self-interest as well as, for some, a conviction that it was the moral and egalitarian thing to do. The conservative *New York Times* argued against raising black troops simply to prove blacks would fight or for the purpose of "loosing an ethnological knot" but supported their use for "its immediate effects . . . on the fortunes of war." Governor Andrew engaged the services of his friend John Forbes to lobby Washington in early January for the inclusion of blacks in the army. On January 22 Forbes reported the good news that "our Rulers . . . seem at last open to the necessity of using the negro for our own salvation first and secondly for his own." Four days later Secretary of War Edwin M. Stanton authorized Andrew to raise regiments which "may include persons of African descent, organized into special corps."[1]

Andrew understood the critical importance of making the venture a success, and he staked his reputation and career upon his conviction that blacks would fight and fight well. After all, there were many who hoped the experiment would fail and some who were sure it would. The latter gave several reasons: a rebellion by whites should be put down by whites; blacks would not enlist; blacks were too cowardly to fight and would run when faced with white Southerners; blacks were not intelligent enough to learn drill; blacks with guns would return to the savage instincts of the jungle; Southerners would become more determined to keep up the fight; white soldiers would not serve alongside black soldiers; blacks would demoralize white soldiers. Andrew determined to prove the error in these objections. Frederick Douglass too was countering these racist notions and trying to persuade uncertain Northern whites of the rightness of the venture. In a speech in New York on February 6, Douglass gave witness that "the colored man only waits for admission into the service of his country. . . . They are ready to rally under the stars and stripes at the first tap of the drum. Give them a chance; stop calling them 'niggers,' and call them soldiers." The experiment was about to begin.[2]

 God's Work

GIVEN THE POLITICAL DELICACY of the situation, Andrew carefully selected white officers who had proven themselves in battle and who came from powerful and respected families with antislavery convictions secure enough to deflect the criticism and pressure of accepting such a position. Also, with the enormous costs of raising a regiment, private sector backing and contributions were highly desirable. Sons of wealthy families with good connections would ease the strain. Andrew again turned for help to Forbes, who responded with two names: Captain Norwood Penrose Hallowell of the Twentieth Massachusetts Infantry and Captain Robert Gould Shaw. Both candidates had joined the war from the start and had been tested in battles, including the war's bloodiest day at Antietam. Hallowell's father, Morris, was a wealthy Philadelphia merchant, Quaker, and longtime abolitionist who used his resources to establish a hospital for recuperating soldiers. Norwood's brother Richard had married the granddaughter of famous antislavery advocates James and Lucretia Mott and had personally traveled to Virginia in 1859, bringing John Brown's body north for burial. Forbes favored Hallowell. "He is a born leader," Forbes wrote the governor, "He has *convictions*." [1]

Andrew considered the choices. He knew Morris Hallowell, but he also knew the Shaws. After listening to Forbes about the strengths and weaknesses of each, Andrew opted for the one with the better family connections. He decided to write Francis Shaw to inform him of his decision to offer Robert the command of the new regiment. That move not only showed political shrewdness, it indicated that Forbes and Andrew were not certain Robert measured up to the difficult task that lay ahead. One way to strengthen the hand that offered the commission was to apply pressure through a family long committed to ending slavery.

Francis and Sarah Shaw read and joyfully reread the governor's letter explaining his choice of their son to head the country's first regiment of Northern black soldiers. Andrew flattered and appealed, spoke of his own "deep conviction," and made it impossible for them to deny him their Robert. He called this "the most important corps" yet organized, "a model for all future colored regiments" whose "success or . . . failure will go far to elevate or depress the estimation in which the character of the colored Americans will be held throughout the world." To command this vanguard unit, Andrew wanted a gentleman "of the highest tone and honor" from the "circles of educated, antislavery society." Andrew observed that antislavery groups had the most at stake in the unit, next to blacks themselves.[2]

Abolitionists had been ridiculed for years as fanatic dreamers; now they had the chance to prove they had been right all along. The governor offered a challenge to the family's honor when he admonished that if Shaw could not "enter upon it [leadership of a black regiment] with a full sense of its importance, with an earnest determination for its success" and with family encouragement, then he should not take it. He brought out their competitive fire by telling them of others who wanted the position. He sealed their support by asking them as "ardent, faithful, and true Republicans and friends of liberty" who "have always contributed to the strength and healing of our generation" to demonstrate those qualities again. Significantly, Andrew had not sent the offer directly to Captain Shaw, but had enclosed it in a separate envelope with his letter to Francis. Andrew was still unsure of the depth of Shaw's commitment to abolition; otherwise he would have corresponded directly, man to man, not man through father to son. The governor asked his friend to forward the offer to Shaw, because he knew that the son would have a hard time refusing the father. Andrew closed by pleading, "If in any way, by suggestion or otherwise, you can aid the purpose . . . of this letter [you will have my] heartiest gratitude."[3]

Francis left immediately to hand-carry the unparalleled offer to his son. Finding Robert in the Army of the Potomac's winter camp at Stafford Court House, Virginia, Shaw took him to a quiet spot and gave him Andrew's letter. The fact that the governor had placed his confidence in the father's ability to persuade can be seen in the letter to the son. Andrew felt no need to flatter or elucidate the arguments:

Captain,

I am about to organize in Massachusetts a Colored Regiment as part of the volunteer quota of this State—the commissioned officers to be white men. I have today written your Father expressing to him my sense of the importance of this undertaking, and requesting him to forward to you this letter, in which I offer to you the Commission of Colonel over it. The Lieutenant Colonelcy I have offered to Captain Hallowell of the Twentieth Massachusetts Regiment. It is important to the organization of this regiment that I should receive your reply to this offer at the earliest day consistent with your ability to arrive at a deliberate conclusion on the subject.

Respectfully and very truly yours,
John A. Andrew[4]

Andrew might have expected that the father would personally deliver the letter, but just in case he did not, the governor made certain that Shaw knew that his parents had been informed. Psychologically, this would make the parents partners in the offer and make it difficult for a son to refuse.

But Shaw did refuse, thinking the position "anything but an agreeable task." His father tried not to pressure him, but his presence surely indicated his feelings. Shaw had been through a lot with his regiment, and seen many of his friends die near him. He was loyal to their memory and to the men who remained to fight on future fields. He discussed the offer with his close friend and tentmate Charles Morse, who wondered with him whether the position might be ridiculed, doubted that blacks would enlist, and questioned the fighting ability of black troops. Morse felt so strongly about the Second that he told Shaw he would never leave it.[5]

Shaw sought the opinions of other officers, most of whom hated to see him leave the regiment. Some of them reminded him that he had just declined a good position with the Second Massachusetts Cavalry, a unit being formed under his sister Josephine's fiancé, Charles Russell Lowell. The two fellow officers who could have provided Shaw the most support, Morris Copeland and James Savage, were no longer around to help him decide. Shaw's best friends from the Second, his cousin Harry Russell, Copeland, Savage, Morse, Greely Curtis, and Dr. Lincoln Stone, all held antislavery views, but only Copeland and Savage were ardent abolitionists. Months before Andrew's offer, Copeland had talked with Savage and Shaw about starting a black regiment, not only to "sever the connection between master and slave, but . . . aid the race in its own regeneration." Savage agreed to join such a unit. Copeland had taken Shaw with him to Washington in May 1862 to ask permission of Secretary of War Stanton to raise a regiment of black soldiers. Copeland had convinced Shaw by telling him, "The raising of black regiments will be an era in our history, and the greatest thing that has been done for the negro race." With Copeland in the lead and before the Second had been in a major battle, Shaw had agreed to transfer to this unit with the rank of major. But the plan was rejected. After Copeland continued "fuming and raging" about slavery and published an open letter in a Boston paper asking Stanton to reconsider using blacks as soldiers, Stanton forced him out of the army on grounds of insubordination. It is more than likely that when Governor Andrew first considered those he wanted to head the Fifty-fourth, Copeland stood at the top of the list.[6]

Savage, who was described by Captain Richard Cary of the Second Massachusetts as "quite prominent among the rabid republicans" and as "one of those who came out to whip the rebels [and] free all the niggers," died in October 1862 from wounds received at Cedar Mountain. After Savage's death, Shaw remembered that "Jim's purity, conscientiousness and manliness were well known. . . . The best we can have for a friend is, that he may resemble James Savage." Savage had publicly stated that only one thing could cause him to leave the Second, the raising of a black regiment. Maybe Shaw would have accepted readily had Copeland and Savage been there to offer support, but they were not. And had they been alive, he most likely would not have received the call in the first place.[7]

Shaw pondered and fretted, thought over the "great honour" of the governor's compliment, and the next morning wrote out his refusal. He told his father, "I would take it, if I thought myself equal to the responsibility of such a position." Shaw's father accepted the letter and, leaving to make the heavy-hearted journey to Boston, sent word to Sarah that Robert had refused. In Virginia, Shaw continued to ponder his decision. He may have thought of his words to his mother the previous fall, when she accused him of "degenerating sadly from the principles" by which he was raised. He had responded that he was just "an ordinary mortal." It is highly probable that during his errand Francis Shaw hand-delivered a letter from Sarah to Robert. In it she praised Governor Andrew's offer, then elevated the pressure: "Well! I feel as if God had called you up to a holy work. You helped him at a crisis when the most important question is to be solved that has been asked since the world began. I know the task is arduous . . . but it is God's work." Unconvincingly, Sarah closed by writing, "If you decide no after prayer and thought, I shall feel that you did entirely right."[8]

Shaw believed in abolitionism, but it was his mother's life work. He felt guilty over his lack of commitment. In November 1862 Shaw wrote to Annie of his great love for his mother and of "the sacrifices she has made for me, and for which I can never repay her." Three months later, on the day he rejected the governor, he knew that he also had rejected his mother. Shaw wrote Annie of his decision, telling her, "Mother will think I am shirking my duty." Shaw agonized over what he had done.[9]

Two days later, Francis Shaw received a short telegram that made him proud. Robert had changed his mind and was telling him to destroy the refusal letter. He followed his son's instructions to telegraph Governor Andrew that he accepted the commission. Whether the pressure he felt from home, the memory of his dead friends, his antislavery sympathy, or a chance to be near his mother and Annie while he recruited in Boston had the most influence on his action cannot be known. Perhaps they all pushed and helped him to be courageous.[10]

Years later, in his own interpretation of what happened, the philosopher William James recalled Shaw's special sense of duty. James spoke of the "manly virtues" of courage, battle instinct, and willingness to sacrifice one's "life-blood" on the fields of war. James said most men had this kind of "common and gregarious" courage. But what Shaw did when he left the Second, James continued, showed a higher courage—the "lonely courage" it took to drop "his warm commission in the glorious Second" to lead black troops. James hailed Shaw's courage in leaving a regiment so correct "socially" to throw himself into "this new negro-soldier venture, [where] loneliness was certain, ridicule inevitable, failure possible; and Shaw was only twenty-five."[11]

Governor Andrew got the bad news before he got the good. After Francis telegraphed Sarah, Sarah wrote the governor, told him of her son's rejection, and lamented, "This decision has caused me the bitterest disappointment I have ever experienced." Had Robert accepted, "it would have been the proudest moment of my life and I could have died satisfied that I had not lived in vain. . . . I have shed bitter tears over his refusal." She did not have long to ache. On hearing that Robert changed his mind, she wrote him of her "deep and holy joy" that he had been "willing to take up the cross." She thanked him: "God rewards a hundred-fold every good aspiration of his children. . . . Now I feel ready to die, for I see you willing to give y[ou]r support to the cause of truth that is lying crushed and bleeding." For his part, Andrew worried a bit about Shaw and tried to get him to accept the lieutenant colonelcy. If Shaw accepted this change, Andrew would hand the command of the regiment to Hallowell, who had had no misgivings, had responded immediately, and was on his way to Boston to begin recruiting. But Shaw held on to the original offer, took the colonelcy, and soon proved to Andrew the correctness of his trust.[12]

In addition to the praise he received from his mother and the governor for taking the position, Shaw received accolades from many sources. Before he made the trip to Boston, he rode with Charles Morse to talk with their friend Greely Curtis, now with the First Massachusetts Cavalry. Curtis lived with another of Shaw's friends who had joined the Second at its formation, Henry Lee Higginson. Higginson recalled that what Shaw told them was "great news, indeed a real event in all our lives; for we all knew how much Robert cared for his own regiment, . . . how fond he was of his old comrades, and how contrary to his wishes this move was." Curtis and Higginson told Shaw they were proud of him and approved his decision. On February 12 Shaw received a letter from an officer he barely knew but who had been talking with Morse: "Rest assured you have done a good thing. I could not myself do what you and Hallowell have done, and so I respect it the more." This officer went on to tell him it was natural to be scared, and that one day history will "justify your course" and "all will confess that you were right, and wonder how the world could have been so wrong." Bolstered by this welcome support, and believing that most officers favored arming blacks, Shaw reached New York on February 11. After receiving what must have been exhausting and irresistible praise and teary-eyed expressions of love from his mother, Shaw left for Boston on the fourteenth to organize the new regiment.[13]

18 Men of Color, To Arms!

GOVERNOR ANDREW LEFT very little to chance for his "design and hope to make this a model regiment." Even before Shaw arrived, Andrew put together a special "Black Committee" to advise, recruit, and raise money. Andrew knew that if blacks failed to pick up the gauntlet and volunteer, whites would further stereotype them as cowardly. Even before Anna Shaw heard that her brother would head the regiment, she wrote her cousin Mimi (Captain Russell's sister) and worried, "I wonder if they will enlist. They would have a year ago but I have heard that a good many have felt very indignant at being excluded & say that they will not go now. I hope that is not so." Writing to his mother on February 4, Charles Russell Lowell feared that "the blacks here [in Boston] are too comfortable to do anything more than talk about freedom." But Shaw's appointment and Andrew's committee changed Lowell's assessment: "I think it very good of Shaw (who is not at all a fanatic) to undertake the thing. . . . You see this is likely to be a success, if any black regiment can be a success." [1]

Many prominent blacks did speak out against enlistment. They were angry that the unit would have no black officers and that the government had turned to them to fight when they were not allowed to vote or hold office in most Northern states. One prominent black voice, William Wells Brown, demanded "equality first, guns afterward." Another, Henry Highland Garnet, questioned the North's sincerity, asking aloud, "What have black men to fight for in this war?" Andrew heard the dissenters and told the committee to get to work and "awaken interest" among the black community. On February 17, at a war meeting at the Joy Street Baptist Church, a crowd of black Bostonians heard speakers who implored them to join the army. Wendell Phillips, whom many recognized as a longtime friend of equality and who was known as the "golden trumpet of abolition" for his stinging oratory, acknowledged the injustice of not being able to have black officers but asked, "If you cannot have a whole loaf, will you not take a slice? That is the great question for you to decide." Soon many decided to grasp the slice; they would try for more later. [2]

Andrew named George L. Stearns to head the committee on recruiting. Stearns was a wealthy manufacturer of lead pipe from

Medford, Massachusetts, who became an active abolitionist after he married a niece of Lydia Maria Child. Unitarian in belief, Stearns wore an imposing chest-length brown beard that made him look like an Old Testament Moses. Never flinching in his conviction that slavery should be destroyed at any cost, he had purchased and sent rifles to the free-soilers of Kansas in the 1850s. As a member of the "Secret Six," he financed John Brown's raid on Harper's Ferry in 1859. Historian William S. McFeely summed up Stearns's interest in the Fifty-fourth as "making good on his mentor's promise of raising an insurrection." Other members of the committee included the ubiquitous John Forbes, who had met with Brown but had not helped him financially; Norwood Hallowell's brother Richard, from Boston; James B. Congdon, a prominent merchant of New Bedford; businessmen Amos Adams Lawrence, William I. Bowditch, and LeBaron Russell of Boston; Willard Phillips of Salem; and Francis Shaw.[3]

All of these members actively raised money and helped recruit. They paid for scores of advertisements in many newspapers. One such ad, of February 16 in Boston papers, called: "To COLORED MEN! Wanted—Good men for the 54th Regiment of Massachusetts Volunteers, of African descent, Col. Robert G. Shaw. . . . All necessary information can be obtained at the Office corner of Cambridge and North Russell streets. Lieut. J. W. M. Appleton, Recruiting Officer." Another focused on honor and racial equality: "Colored Men Attention! Colored Men, Rally around the Flag of Freedom and evince that you are not inferior in Courage and Patriotism to White Men. An opportunity is now being afforded to Colored Men to prove their Manhood and Loyalty by enlisting in the 54th Regiment." By February 13 the committee circulated a "Subscription Paper" which asked for help in establishing the new regiment. The paper ran a middle course of not mentioning black freedom or moral arguments. Instead, it focused on the common though prejudiced belief that blacks had an advantage when fighting "in a Southern climate." The paper reminded readers that black soldiers would "reduce the number" of white replacements required to bolster dwindling armies. Most members of the committee opened the drive by pledging themselves to five hundred dollars each. Abolitionist leader Gerrit Smith of New York added five hundred more, and the "friends of F.G. Shaw" gave fourteen hundred dollars. In the end almost every abolitionist in Boston had anted up between twenty and five hundred dollars.[4]

While his comrades raised money—over a hundred thousand dollars—Stearns took to the road to do most of the legwork in raising the regiment. He established a central recruiting office in Buffalo and successfully implored black leaders to hold recruiting meetings. He told them the state legislature had appropriated funds to remunerate recruiters two dollars for each recruit and would pay each recruit a fifty-dollar bounty for enlisting, after the regiment mustered into service. The committee would absorb the transportation costs to camp, and then, if the enlistee was rejected by the surgeon there, would pay return costs. The state promised to give eight dollars a month to families left behind. Local communities could help with enlistment bonuses and additional bounties. The men would be paid thirteen dollars a month, the same as white privates. Now was the time to help themselves and their race and to support old John Brown. While many black leaders had initially spoken out against the regiment, most changed their minds and joined with those who argued that they must act now or forever lose their chance.[5]

The recruiters who threw themselves behind the Fifty-fourth included many of the leaders of mid-nineteenth-century black America: William Wells Brown, John S. Rock, Charles Lenox Remond, Martin R. Delany, John Jones, Robert Purvis, O. S. B. Wall, Henry Highland Garnet, and John Mercer Langston. They spoke from church pulpits, on street corners, or added their voices to the call for men being advertised in over one hundred Northern news-papers. Stearns knew whom to call on first. Without delay, as his first stop on a long trip, he went to Rochester to ask his friend Frederick Douglass for the help he knew Douglass would give. Three weeks before this, the great orator told an audience, "The paper proclamation must now be made iron, lead, and fire, by the prompt employment of the negro's arm in the contest." Douglass proved his support by enrolling his sons Lewis and Charles into the regiment and publishing, in the March issue of *Douglass's Monthly*, the famous editorial "Men of Color to Arms!" Then this most famous of black leaders canvassed western New York to en-courage black men to fight. In all, Douglass sent over one hundred men into the regiment. Stearns and the others ensured that this "new negro-soldier venture" would succeed.[6]

 The Officers

WHILE STEARNS WORKED his way through the Midwest and Canada seeking help and enrolling men, Shaw selected officers. He understood his mission and told Annie, "What I have to do is to prove that a negro can be made a good soldier." His first real job was to pick dedicated men, not just seekers of higher rank. The governor's one order to Shaw was that all officers had to be from Massachusetts. Shaw had a relatively easy job, since he had more applicants than positions and the governor and Norwood Hallowell had already made some key selections. Of the original twenty-nine officers appointed, fourteen came from three-year regiments, eight from nine-month units, one from the militia, and the rest from civilian jobs. Most of them had been enlisted men, but only half a dozen had prior service as officers. Governor Andrew selected Norwood Hallowell's brother, Lieutenant Edward Needles Hallowell of the Twentieth Massachusetts, to be third in command, with the rank of major. Forbes had recommended him for the position because of his reputation as "a tip top man, a regular Negrophile."[1]

Other abolition-minded men were selected for the officer corps. Most of them had a much more egalitarian sense of their cause than did Shaw, who often referred to himself as "a Nigger Colonel" and to his regiment as "a good nigger concern" or "darky concern." John W. M. Appleton, a skinny hometown boy with outward-turning ears and a longish neck on a narrow frame, had served some garrison duty in Boston Harbor until his discharge in 1862. Then, stirred by what he called the "Glorious Proclamation of our President," he sought reenlistment. In January, Appleton applied for a commission with Colonel Thomas W. Higginson—a member of the "Secret Six" supporters of John Brown—who was recruiting a regiment from among the runaway and freed slaves in South Carolina. Appleton told Higginson, "The two great problems that demand our attention in connection with the freedom of the slave are Firstly will the freedman work for his living? Secondly will he fight for his liberty? I believe that he will do both and I desire to assist him to do the latter." Notably, the powerful George Stearns recommended him to Higginson in a letter of January 20. Higginson promptly offered Appleton a commission, but by that time—and because of the timing involved with mail delivery—Appleton had already accepted another with the Fifty-fourth. He busied himself recruiting in Cambridge, looking for and enrolling the one hundred men for what became Company A.[2]

William H. Simpkins, a handsome clerk from West Roxbury who was serving as a sergeant in the Forty-fourth Massachusetts, became the captain of Company K. A thoughtful man, Simpkins related his reason for joining the enterprise: "This is no hasty conclusion, no blind leap of an enthusiast, but the result of much hard thinking. It will not be at first, and probably not for a long time, an agreeable position, for many reasons too evident to state. . . . Then this is nothing but an experiment after all; but it is an experiment that I think it is high time we should try." Twenty-three-year-old Simpkins would die near Shaw on the rampart at Fort Wagner five months later.[3]

By the end of March, Shaw had added his choices to those already comissioned. Garth Wilkinson "Wilkie" James, the younger brother of William and Henry James, had learned from his parents that "slavery was a monstrous wrong, its destruction worthy of a man's best effort, even unto the laying down of life." James's father said that Wilkie was "vastly attached to the negro-soldier cause; believes . . . that the world has existed for it." Wilkie and his buddy Cabot Russel, both of the Forty-fourth Massachusetts, applied for commissions, and Shaw quickly accepted them. Years later, James remembered that many of the men of the Forty-fourth gave them "sharp rebukes" for joining in this "crazy scheme." The stern-faced, blond-haired Russel, who had slept since 1859 with a portrait of John Brown above his bed and had deserted from his freshman year at Harvard in 1862 to join the Forty-fourth, gleefully hoped for "the power of darkness" to help win the war. At Fort Wagner the nineteen-year-old James suffered severe wounds, and Russel, eighteen years old, was killed.[4]

In addition to Simpkins, James, and Russel, Shaw raided the Forty-fourth for Charles Tucker, Willard Howard, Henry Little-field, Edward Jones, and George Pope. Not only were they available, but they already knew one another—a situation that would strengthen their commitment to their fellow officers and speed the training of the regiment. One of the officers remembered "that we were selected to try a most important experiment, an experiment which must not fail." Shaw did not pull men from his old regiment, the Second, probably out of loyalty to the unit. However, he did persuade his close friend, Dr. Lincoln Stone, to transfer to the Fifty-fourth to inspect all the recruits to guarantee their health and physical aptitude. But regardless of who got selected, Shaw insisted, "I don't want to take any one whom I don't know myself." [5]

20 The Recruits

SHAW WOULD ORGANIZE and drill the regiment at Camp Meigs, located in Readville, just southwest of Boston on the Boston and Providence Railroad. Norwood Hallowell opened the camp on February 21 by reporting to the commandant, Brigadier General R. A. Peirce. While Hallowell took charge at the facility, Stearns, Douglass, and others continued to look for men. John Mercer Langston scoured Ohio, Indiana, and Illinois for recruits and sent to Camp Meigs several hundred "of the very best young colored men" who understood "the dignity, responsibility and danger of their position." One Xenia, Ohio, mother told Langston she worried for her son but was proud to see him fight because "liberty is better than life." The young man died at Fort Wagner. James Caldwell, the grandson of Sojourner Truth, came from Battle Creek, Michigan. Among the early enlistments, three fugitive slaves and three emancipated slaves joined the group of fourteen from egalitarian Oberlin, Ohio. Lewis and Charles Douglass arrived in camp in late March with fifty men from western New York. Their famous father accompanied them to Readville. Stephen A. Swails, thirty and married, quit his job as a canal boatman in Elmira, New York, to join the army. He would be promoted to become the regiment's first African American lieutenant in January 1865. [1]

By February 18 Lieutenant James W. Grace had recruited

twenty-seven men in New Bedford. Among the first to join was a former slave from Virginia, William H. Carney. Carney had been born in Norfolk in 1840, the son of William Carney and Ann Dean. Their owner's will freed them in 1854. Two years later, the family left Virginia, having chosen New Bedford over Pennsylvania because, as Carney put it, "the black man was not secure on the soil where the Declaration of Independence was written." Strong and brave, William Carney would become the first African American to win the Medal of Honor. An effervescent, highly literate, twenty-six-year-old seaman named James H. Gooding also cast his lot with the Fifty-fourth. During his time of service, Gooding wrote weekly letters to the *New Bedford Mercury,* keeping the regiment alive for the home folks. Gooding died on July 19, 1864, after spending five months as a prisoner of war at Andersonville, Georgia.[2]

In the middle of March, a recruiting rally in New Bedford induced others to join. Thomas Dawes Eliot, the U.S. congressman representing the city, told the gathering, "This is a war between the principles of slave labor and free labor. . . . They say you have not the courage to fight, that you are not manly enough. They lie! and you will prove it to them." Twenty-four-year-old Wesley Furlong, who had been a steward, appeared at the meeting in a uniform with sergeant's stripes on his sleeves. He told his neighbors, "The black man must put down this war." Furlong wanted to be remembered as one "who fought for the liberty of his race and to prove himself a man." Grace did his job well enough in New Bedford, and a few days after the meeting the town's company, Company C, had eighty members.[3]

The Fifty-fourth had the pick of the Northern black population, as its ranks filled with men who had long awaited the opportunity to fight. In the middle of April, fifty recruits from Buffalo, Cincinnati, and Detroit took a train to New York and transferred to a steamer bound for Boston. An observer claimed that they all could "read and write" and made "an excellent appearance." At one early regimental muster, a newspaperman noted that "408 . . . signed their names in a good and clear hand." Many of the men came from large cities, where they had had more opportunities to attend school and where daily jobs required reading. In Philadelphia, African American recruiting sergeant A. M. Green helped enlist one hundred men into Company B. The men had been carpenters, hotel keepers, barbers, artists, day laborers, and dockworkers. Also in Philadelphia, five-foot-six-inch-tall, light-complected George Stephens usually recruited in churches. But on April 6 he addressed the largest recruiting rally held in the city, telling the listeners, "We do not deserve the name of freemen if we disregard the teachings of the hour and fail to place in the balance against oppression treason and tyranny, our interests, our arms, and our lives." Stephens was as good as his word, joining and being immediately promoted to sergeant, Company B. Overall, given the fact that the Fifty-fourth Massachusetts was the first black regiment raised from an untapped source, it became one of the most physically fit and academically able units to serve during the Civil War.[4]

The oldest man to join, forty-six-year-old Peter Vogelsang, was recommended by Francis Shaw. Vogelsang was known to Shaw's father as a clerk in Brooklyn who very much wanted to fight for his country. Colonel Shaw had originally warned his father that with the rigorous physical tests, "no man of 46 would pass." Three weeks later, Shaw appointed Vogelsang sergeant of Company H and called him "very efficient." By 1865 First Lieutenant Vogelsang was serving as regimental quartermaster and was one of three black men promoted to officer rank within the Fifty-fourth. Altogether, thirty-eight men over forty years old served with the regiment.[5]

Robert Gould Shaw on the occasion of his wedding
and promotion to colonel, May 1863. Boston Athenaeum.

Sarah Blake Sturgis Shaw, mother of
Robert Gould Shaw, circa 1861.
Staten Island Institute of Arts and Sciences.

Francis George Shaw, father of
Robert Gould Shaw, 1863.
Staten Island Institute of Arts and Sciences.

Josephine "Effie" Shaw, Robert Gould Shaw's sister, with her fiancé,
Lieutenant Colonel Charles Russell Lowell, Sixth U.S. Cavalry, 1863.
From Edward Emerson, *Life and Letters of Charles Russell Lowell*
(Boston: Houghton Mifflin, 1907).

Annie Kneeland Haggerty Shaw,
wife of Robert Gould Shaw, May 1863.
Boston Athenaeum.

Shaw with close friends of the Second Massachusetts Infantry who actively supported raising an army of black soldiers: from left, James Savage, Jr., Shaw, R. Morris Copeland, and Henry S. Russell. MOLLUS-Mass. Collection, USAMHI.

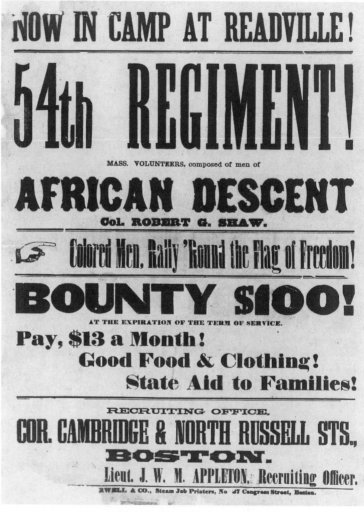

The first recruiting poster for the Fifty-fourth Massachusetts Infantry, February 1863. Massachusetts Historical Society.

Captain John W. M. Appleton, recruiter for the
Fifty-fourth Massachusetts Infantry. MOLLUS-Mass.
Collection, USAMHI.

Lieutenant Peter Vogelsang, at age forty-six
the oldest man to join the Fifty-fourth Massachusetts Infantry.
MOLLUS-Mass. Collection, USAMHI.

Private Abraham F. Brown,
Fifty-fourth Massachusetts
Infantry, killed at James
Island, South Carolina,
July 11, 1863. Massachusetts
Historical Society.

Lewis H. Douglass (son of Frederick Douglass),
regimental sergeant-major, Fifty-fourth
Massachusetts Infantry. Frederick Douglass
Collection, Box 28-10 Photo Album, Moorland-
Spingarn Research Center, Howard University.

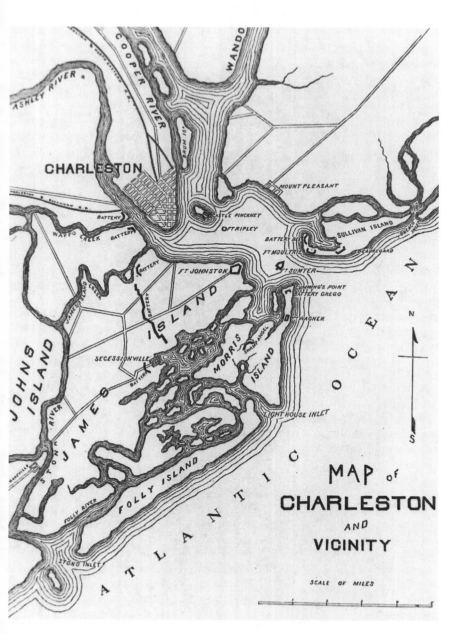

Map of Charleston, South Carolina, showing Morris Island and Fort Wagner.
From *The Soldiers in Our Civil War* (1884). By permission of the
New Bedford Whaling Museum.

Charlotte Forten, Beaufort schoolteacher
and friend of Robert Gould Shaw, circa 1863.
Library of Congress.

Colonel James M. Montgomery,
commander of the Second South Carolina
Infantry. Kansas State Historical Society,
Topeka, Kansas.

Battlefield sketch of Fort Wagner, July 19, 1863, by Frank Vizetelly, with inscription: "In the ditch, they lay piled, negroes & whites, four & five deep on each other, there could not have been less than 250 in the moat, some partially submerged." By permission of Houghton Library, Harvard University.

Veterans of the Fifty-fourth Massachusetts at the unveiling of the
Augustus Saint-Gaudens Memorial, Boston Common, May 31, 1897.
Massachusetts Historical Society.

21 Camp Meigs

MOST RECRUITS ARRIVED by train to the Readville station and marched or walked the four hundred yards to Camp Meigs, where they presented themselves to the guard. The officer of the day scrutinized their enlistment papers and signed them in. Immediately thereafter they were taken to the camp infirmary, where they met a gravelly-voiced man with a moderate brown and gray beard, long bushy eyebrows, and soft hands. Dr. Lincoln Ripley Stone, of Salem, had seen it all in his two years with the Second Massachusetts. He knew the shirkers who feigned sickness at the edge of battle, the too-young hopefuls who sought to enlist even if underaged, and the casualties of war. Stone knew firsthand the horrors of war from attending the wounded, dying, and dead soldiers of the Army of the Potomac. He also knew too well that since Massachusetts paid recruiters two dollars for each recruit accepted, many mercenary recruiters sent along every available body to the regiments. Since accepting his friend Shaw's offer to join the Fifty-fourth Massachusetts, Stone set out to ensure that only the most physically fit African Americans gained enlistment. A curious job, the selection of those most able to die in combat. With a serious manner and an inquisitive nature, Stone administered a rigorous examination to every aspirant.[1]

For most of them, this was their second physical. In order to save the costs of transporting unsuitable men both ways, the Black Committee hired contract physicians throughout the North. These doctors examined recruits in the town where they signed enlistment papers. Even with this precautionary screening, Dr. Stone rejected many aspiring soldiers—they would have to find another regiment that had less on the line than the North's showcase unit.

When some complained that perhaps the exams were set at an even higher standard at Readville, Shaw reassured his father, "In my opinion Dr. Stone is not too strict in his examinations. In fact I have continually urged him to be particular—and the committee here have complained of it very much." Shaw insisted on quality and told his father, "We are picking them carefully & shall have a very sound set." He explained further that "to accept a man who is doubtful, is, in my opinion, cheating the Government, wronging the man, & harming the regiment." Adjutant Wilkie James surmised that enough men had been rejected to field another entire regiment. James Gooding of Company C wrote home as early as March 23 to report, pridefully, that 132 of 500 men had been rejected by Stone. William Schouler, the adjutant general of Massachusetts, recorded that every third man failed. Perhaps Shaw and Stone abused their power to choose or deny men; but they constructed the most highly selective regiment of the war. The regiment was healthier than most and stayed that way, because chronic sufferers had been rejected, although, naturally, men caught colds and a few died of bronchitis, pneumonia, and smallpox. No doctor's or colonel's precautions could stop the spread of camp and campaign afflictions. Notwithstanding the actual percentage of volunteers rejected—and dejected—those who passed were quickly made to look like soldiers.[2]

Norwood Hallowell described the change: "Upon arrival they were marched to the neighboring pond, disrobed, washed and uniformed. Their old clothes were burnt. The transformation was quite wonderful. The recruit was very much pleased with the uniform. He straightened up, grew inches taller, lifted not shuffled, his feet, began at once to try, and to try hard, to take the position of the soldier." Every day, Shaw and Hallowell oversaw the repetition of this process as new recruits arrived at Readville. Two days after camp opened, Shaw told Charles Morse that he had thirty men at Readville "all washed & uniformed. They feel as big as all creation—and really look very well." By the end of the first week, February 28, seventy-two men had started to become soldiers. After that, as Shaw recalled, recruits came in "every day." Throughout the time at Camp Meigs, on average, twelve men daily discarded their civilian clothes for the blue uniforms of the Union.[3]

The regiment was assigned to occupy ten wooden barracks, each housing one hundred men. There was a separate barracks for the officers and a cook house. Beginning the daily schedule, reveille shook the men awake at 5:30, and they quickly formed for roll call. Shaw ordered the officers to "see that the men stand at attention while in the ranks." After all were accounted for, they cleaned the barracks, aired their bedding, and dressed for breakfast at 7:00. Half an hour later, Stone held sick call and the men took in their bedding and prepared the barracks for inspection. The regiment reformed at 8:00 to begin drill instruction. For the first weeks of camp, snow stood deep on the ground and prevented full regimental and company drills, so Shaw ordered the men instructed by squads inside empty barracks. He ordered the officers: "Particular attention should be paid to the soldierly bearing of the men, and their steadiness in the ranks." After the snow melted, Shaw sent the men outdoors, drilling them at least five hours per day. Under an order specifying "no excuses," corporals and sergeants took special instruction on drill and tactics from the senior captain, Alfred S. Hartwell. Some days, long marches with full packs helped build up the men's endurance and confidence. With lunch, supper, and inspections, the men had little time for anything other than the rigorous training schedule. Tattoo ordered the men into bed at 8:00 P.M. Thirty minutes later, taps blew lights out and quieted all talking and singing in the barracks.[4]

Shaw did what he could to provide for the comfort of his men. Recruits who came in too late to see Stone and visit the pond still found, in the words of Gooding, "a nice warm fire and a good supper." First Lieutenant John Ritchie, the regimental quartermaster and a former Harvard classmate of Shaw's, worked hard to keep the men supplied with the appropriate military gear. Two days before camp opened, Ritchie had requisitioned and received the "necessaries" for a hundred men: 100 woolen blankets, rubber blankets, bedsacks, overcoats, uniform coats, sack coats, pants, and pairs of shoes; and 200 shirts, pairs of underwear, and pairs of socks. The day camp opened, he had 25 cords of wood ready to warm the barracks. Every week, Ritchie received similar items from General Peirce, plus badges of rank, drums, fifes, kettles, mess packs, flannel shirts, forage caps, haversacks, canteens, 3 wall tents, 522 shelter tents, and 4 hospital tents. As the governor's "model" regiment, the men were well supplied and cared for by the state. Everything was first rate, as Shaw's regiment got the newest and the best of everything in quantities that made them want for nothing. Shaw kept a sharp eye focused on making every man and every detail as nearly perfect as possible so that no critic could complain about slovenliness. The men did, however, have to drill through the winter with old muskets, having to wait until 1,000 Enfield rifles became available in May.[5]

Shaw understood the risks. Any misstep would be used to embarrass those who already were being ridiculed for believing that blacks would fight. He would impose the strict discipline he had been subjected to while in the Second Massachusetts and draw from his coming of age under watchful eyes of Jesuits and Monsieur Roulet. He believed strongly that most enlisted men acted in excess unless restrained by the educated and civilized officer ranks. Often Shaw wrote of the superiority of strictly managed regiments over those with lax standards. He was sure that a soldier's behavior in battle "depends almost entirely on the discipline." Shaw emulated General George B. McClellan, who had turned the disorderly recruits of 1861 into a professional army. But Shaw also believed he had different material than did McClellan. Shaw was a paternalist, not at all sure that the detractors were incorrect about blacks' abilities. Still he could not show those reservations to his men or to outsiders. He understood that in these early stages, appearances meant everything. Shaw insisted that all company commanders personally inspect every soldier who wanted to leave the base to ensure that that man was "neatly dressed in his uniform & in fine weather with his boots blacked." [6]

Yet, in an effort to prevent ridicule and instill discipline, Shaw went too far, invoking the letter of military law without leeway for particulars. For a minor disturbance, Shaw put the offenders in the guard house, chains, and worse. When men quarreled with officers, Shaw threatened them with death. He forced men to stand on barrels for hours, promising them a worse punishment if they fell to fatigue. Others were gagged with their hands and feet bound together, their arms stretched around heavy sticks. These methods were all commonly used punishments during the war; but Shaw pushed the measures beyond propriety. When his mother asked him about "complaints from outsiders of undue severity" being gossiped around, Shaw defended himself, "I shall continue to do what I know is right in that particular, and . . . any reports of cruelty, are entirely untrue." [7]

Even the officers were not exempt from Shaw's harsh standards. Captain Appleton complained to his wife about the "very stringent discipline. In fact I have never known a Regiment where the officers were under as strict discipline as the 54th." Undoubtedly too, Shaw's tough demands made his officers stricter on the men. Norwood Hallowell recalled that Shaw punished in accord with what white soldiers received "in all well-disciplined regiments." He labeled Shaw's technique "the method of coercion, and it was successful." However, at the time of Hallowell's assessment, Shaw had become a martyr to the cause and Hallowell was loyal to his memory. The records are incomplete about the exact punishments inflicted, but they were harsh enough that the camp commandant, General Peirce, called them "contrary" to what the army permitted. Peirce had seen many regiments formed and drilled at Meigs and had seen nothing like the punishments inflicted on African American soldiers. Without citing particulars, Peirce ordered Shaw to stop any and all "severe and unusual punishments not laid down by regulations." Undeniably, Shaw was overbearing, but outward appearances were good. And as to punishment, one witness reported, "The guard house is seldom occupied." With the regiment's high profile, a full prison would only be a target for abuse by those who already defamed the Fifty-fourth. Shaw knew that once winter turned to spring, many visitors would come to see the regiment; he must instill order before that happened. He had learned well the lessons that good soldiers were built upon the bedrock of training, discipline, and leadership. The regiment benefited from his adherence to military verities.[8]

In camp the few recruits who couldn't read took reading lessons offered by volunteer teachers. The men increased their dedication to one another through play. After drill many sang, played instruments, and danced in the barracks. Often they picked sides for football. They took pride in themselves and in their mission and tried to get others to join them. Corporal Gooding made a plea to black women to "drive all these young loungers [who have not joined us] off to the war, and if they don't go, say, 'I'm no more gal of thine.'" Attending to their spiritual needs, African American ministers William Jackson and William Grimes, both of New Bedford, competed for congregations and held prayer services in the barracks each evening. The Reverend Mr. Jackson performed at least eight marriage services at the camp. As in armies across centuries, the soldiers looked forward to mail call, when letters or packages poured in from wives and brothers, girlfriends and parents, and various benevolent groups.[9]

Still, as in every regiment in every war, some felt they had made a mistake by joining, a few believed they had been disciplined unfairly, and others were overcome by homesickness or news of trouble at home. Some of the married men had endangered their families' already tenuous economic positions by sacrificing to fight against slavery; bad news from home caused discontent and desertion. Some men had trouble getting along in the closeness of the barracks, others fought with their comrades, and a few could stay no longer.[10]

Deserters were a fact of life among Civil War armies, and the desertion rate for black soldiers exactly mirrored that of white soldiers; but desertion created a special problem among this vanguard black regiment because of the belief that blacks were cowards. On April 24 Shaw told his father, "They are beginning to desert. There are 17–20 absent without leave. None caught yet." The next day Shaw hired a detective to help locate the runaways.[11]

Shaw also ordered his officers to round up the slackers. Captain Appleton remembered going on several expeditions to capture those absent without leave. Once he and Lieutenant Russel found two men in Dedham "and after a little fracas . . . marched them back over the road ironed together. Cabot Russel and I arm in arm, together behind them. Cabot quoting Shakespeare." One snowy night Appleton tracked down eighteen-year-old Charles Draper, whom he found after climbing up a water pipe and looking into a window of a house in Boston. When Appleton called for Draper, "two stout negroes" obstructed him. The captain recalled, "I put my foot in the opening and pointed a pistol at the men . . . they gave way." He found the private under a pile of clothing. Draper would desert again, this time successfully, in April 1864. Another time, Appleton found two of his men in a room with two women. After a scuffle over his pistol, Appleton marched the men to the train station for return to Readville.[12]

Besides the problem of desertion, two scandals received some attention. Word reached the governor that the Reverend Mr. Jackson and other clergymen had induced soldiers to get married to white women, "some of them worthless characters," just to get the fee from the men. In turn, the women were induced by false promises "that they could draw the State Aid." In fact, Massachusetts would not pay aid to women who married soldiers, if the men had married after enlisting. Although some of the accusations were probably true, Jackson, who, on March 10, 1863, became the army's first official black chaplain, adamantly maintained his innocence: "I have never married any white and colored people together on this ground. Neither have I persuaded any persons to get married for the sake of getting the state aid, or bounty." The other scandal happened after the men were paid the fifty-dollar bounty for enlisting. James Gooding said that most men sent the money home, but peddlers "are reaping a rich harvest" by selling jewelry at inflated prices and four-dollar boots for twice that. Norwood Hallowell called these reports "greatly exaggerated." Shaw had ordered that no peddlers be allowed among the men. He told the men to send their money home or put it into a bank. Hallowell admitted that even with these precautions some men had been deceived. Fortunately, these scandals caused only minor flaps and truly were insignificant.[13]

22 A Racial Education

SHAW LEFT THE SECOND with reservations about the competence of black men to become soldiers. His early letters from Readville to his friends show that he still had misgivings as he referred to the black recruits as "niggers" and "darkeys"—terms he avoided in his letters to his mother. Shaw made many racist remarks based upon stereotypes of physical characteristics, particularly the commonly held and scientifically "proven" anthropometric measurement of racial differences in the length of heels. At Harvard, Shaw had listened to Professor Louis Agassiz lecture on and promote these theories of difference, theories that tried to establish a heirarchy of races. Shaw noted that among the heels he observed, "some of them are wonder-ful in that line. One man has them so long that they actually prevent him from making the facings properly." He ridiculed the men's poor language or their mimicking of whites, telling his close friend Charley Morse, "It is very laughable to hear the sergeants explain the drill to the men, as they use words long enough for a Doctor of Divinity or anything else."[1]

Two weeks later, on March 14, Shaw told Annie that everything "is going on prosperously. . . . [The] men are very satisfactory. . . . [and] will be more soldierly" than most American volunteers. He particularly cited Company C from New Bedford as "a very fine body of men, and out of forty, only two cannot read and write. Their barracks are in better order, and more cleanly [kept], than the quarters of any volunteer regiment I have seen in this country." By the end of March, Shaw admitted to his mother, "The intelligence of the men is a great surprise to me"; meanwhile he was telling A. A. Lawrence, "I am perfectly astonished at the general intelligence these darkeys display." Of course Shaw was politic enough to use different language with different listeners. He knew that Lawrence, Forbes, and other influential men on the Black Committee held racist views. For example, the ultrapowerful Forbes often spoke of the regiment at Readville as "the colored children at camp Africa." Shaw tried to please all his supporters and family.[2]

Never before around African Americans, Shaw changed through contact with them. He still held himself superior to blacks and addressed them formally—the way a strict officer behaved around any group of men—but he began to respect their abilities and became attached to and defensive of them. Forced by their actions to question, then conquer, his own misconceptions, he bristled if an outsider abused them. Historian William McFeely concluded that Shaw was getting an education in race relations even if he was "ignorant of . . . [and] groping to know the black men who had enlisted." Once those men proved their intelligence, commitment to order, pluck, and adaptability to military life, Shaw began to learn, and in so doing he won the respect of his men. Recruiter William Wells Brown and Corporal Gooding both wrote of the love the men held for their colonel. Although Shaw still wondered what they might do when they reached the battlefield and never fully threw off his notions of racial heirarchies, he finally stopped calling them "niggers."[3]

With the regiment half filled, Shaw was proud but worried. Secretary of War Stanton wanted Governor Andrew to send the available men to North Carolina to join with the contraband regiment being assembled there under Col. Edward Wild. Shaw protested that "the moral effect on the people at home, of seeing a well-armed, well-drilled, and well-disciplined regiment march, will be lost entirely." He said that they had not yet been supplied with rifles, so no one knew how to use them. That being the case, the men would look foolish in front of white troops in the South. Shaw knew that "it is of much importance to make a favourable impression on the white soldiers from the very beginning." Shaw told Andrew that the regiment would soon be full and should not be sent away piecemeal. If the governor complied with Stanton, Shaw would resign his commission and let Hallowell assume command. The next day Andrew acquiesced, giving Shaw an extra month to get the regiment ready.[4]

By April 6 Shaw was confident enough to invite the public to watch the Fifty-fourth's first dress parade. It was a huge success in educating critics toward the possibility that a black man might be as good a soldier as a white man. Thereafter, Camp Meigs welcomed thousands of well-wishers, scoffers, and curious spectators who usually arrived by train excursion to see the black soldiers. Shaw interacted with "crowds of people . . . every afternoon" and said, "We have heard nothing but words of praise & astonishment from friend & foe—from hunkers & fogeys, old and young." Hallowell remembered that "thousands of strangers" changed their minds after only one visit. Gooding spoke of the "crowds of visitors daily, drawn, no doubt, by the great reputation the regiment is gaining by competency in drill." William Lloyd Garrison and Wendell Phillips regularly took the train to Readville to admire the regiment. Politicians, looking for press opportunities, came to see firsthand how black men looked in blue uniforms. Here was a regiment to be proud of. Gooding gave all the credit to Shaw, "whose quick eye detects anything in a moment out of keeping with order or military discipline." [5]

On May 6, the week before the regiment was filled, Governor Andrew escorted Secretary of the Treasury Salmon P. Chase to see the troops Lincoln had authorized. A soldier remembered this as "a grand gala day" with much cheering and "military spirit." Certainly the feeling of the men improved that day when the quartermaster distributed into each set of eager hands a .577 caliber Enfield rifle. The soldiers promised to "make good use of them." Thoroughly impressed by the unit's abilities, a correspondent for the *Springfield Republican* reported: "Here was a regiment of a thousand men . . . with rather an uncommon amount of muscle. . . . They marched well, they wheeled well, they stood well, they handled their guns well, and there was about their whole array an air of completeness, and order, and morale, such as I have not seen surpassed in any white regiment." The men knew what they were about. They were proud of themselves and took special pride in the designation of the unit as the Fifty-fourth Massachusetts and not the First Colored Infantry. After the War Department established the U.S. Colored Troops, the men of the Fifty-fourth, and those of the soon-to-be raised Fifty-fifth, along with the later-organized Twenty-ninth Connecticut, were the only three Northern black infantry regiments to keep their original designations. It set them apart, and they knew it. They believed all Northern black men would be proud to join them. As Gooding noticed some "strong able-bodied" black men among the visitors, he wondered, "Why are you not here?"[6]

23 Annie Haggerty Shaw

SHAW WAS NOT in camp when Secretary Chase visited; the colonel was on his honeymoon. Since announcing his engagement to Annie Haggerty just days after he accepted command of the Fifty-fourth, Shaw had divided his time between organizing the regiment and courting his fiancée. He absented himself often from the rigors of training to travel to New York or Lenox to be with her. Shaw's mother began to worry that Annie distracted her son from his obligation to the regiment. Sarah told Shaw that he should put off the marriage until after he had devoted himself fully to the Fifty-fourth. But she had deeper objections. Sarah had the motherly love for Robert that one might expect, but she also had always been her son's closest confidant. In that role she spoke to him as a voice of conscience—and he listened.

He always worried what his mother would think. He admired her inner strength and personal confidence—something he and his father had less of. Sarah had always had his deepest love and his earnest ear. When she worried what Annie would do to their relationship, Shaw insisted, "I don't intend to abandon you entirely for Annie!" Jealous, Sarah hated to lose him to another woman. To her, Robert was more than a son. Since his acceptance of the regimental command, he was her John Brown, and she would fight the war vicariously through her son's body. Long committed to moral perfectionism and uplift, Sarah couched her son's work in terms of God's mission: "I see you willing to give y[ou]r support to the cause of truth that is lying crushed and bleeding, I believe the time to be the fulfillment of the Prophecies, & that we are beholding the Second Advent of Christ. . . . I do not fear the lions in y[ou]r path." Sarah brought up her son on principles of abolition; now she believed God had chosen him to strike a blow against the evil slave power. Shaw asked her to "please tell me *exactly* what you think of our being married before I go away?" Sarah responded by expressing her disapproval. Still, Shaw was a grown man and told her, "Excuse me for saying, I didn't think your arguments very powerful." Supporting Sarah, Annie's parents also objected, citing the timing and suggesting postponement.[1]

Shaw answered that the wedding would be held while he was in camp. He swore never to "neglect my duty" because of marriage. He told his mother that he was about "to undertake a very dangerous piece of work" and that he felt "there are more chances than ever of my not getting back." He wanted to be married in case that happened. Shaw did not explain why he felt that way, but the reasons were the same ones that drive people to the altar during every war. After seeing the horrors of battle deaths, Shaw worried more for his own life. Young men often feel invincible, but Shaw had to realize that men much stronger, much "better," than he had been killed right beside him many times. Perhaps Shaw wanted someone to love who was not in danger of an unfriendly bullet—someone beautiful and caring who would write him love letters to comfort him. Philosopher J. Glenn Gray has written that war uproots soldiers from home and community and places them unnaturally in a world of violent men. The rush to the altar in wartime is a grasp for order, moorings, home.[2]

Shaw might have feared that if not now, when?—maybe Annie would not wait for him. Marriage meant the future because of hopes and plans that had to be made and accomplished; it meant that he could not die yet since there was too much to do. Perhaps Shaw feared that he had not checked off "marriage" on the list of life experiences. Maybe he worried that his seed would not be passed to another generation; he was an only son in a nineteenth-century world where it was important to keep the family name, the line, alive. Whatever the reason, he would not be turned away this time. He had taken the regiment for his mother; he would take Annie for himself.

In mid-March, Shaw went to Lenox, picked up his bride-to-be, and took her to Mrs. Crehore's boarding house, only a half mile from camp. Every evening Shaw rode to see her, stayed in the room he occupied beside hers, and got up to be in place for reveille. Shaw spent many happy evenings sitting at Mrs. Crehore's with Annie and with his sister Josephine and her fiancé, Charles Russell Lowell, who both boarded there.[3]

Besides seeing Annie every chance he could, Shaw had become a celebrity in Boston. He spent a lot of time at dinner parties or gatherings where he made short speeches about the progress of making negroes into men, into soldiers, and the prospects of service in the army. He answered a million inane questions about blacks' abilities and began to hate wearing his uniform when away from camp because of the attention he drew. In the worst encounter, he arrived to meet with a ladies' committee which had formed to help the Fifty-fourth. Arriving "with a light heart & jaunty step" and expecting four women, he later told his sister Effie that "stepping into the parlour, a fearful sight met my terrified gaze. There sat what seemed to me, about 17000 ladies & two men. . . . I was brought forward, as to the slaughter, in a terrible perspiration." He took solace in the homes of friends and relatives and proudly admitted being at "a dinner or small party almost every day since I got to Boston, and have enjoyed myself amazingly."[4]

Annie arranged the wedding while he attended to the regiment. Finally bowing to the inevitability of their children's wishes, the families assented to the marriage. It would not be a "Show Wedding" as Sarah had requested. In fact, only a few friends and family assembled for the ceremony at the Protestant Episcopal Church of the Ascension on Fifth Avenue in New York City on May 2. Immediately thereafter, the couple took a train to the summer home of the Haggertys in Lenox. For four days they honeymooned in the Berkshires, taking walks, riding, reading aloud to each other from George Eliot's *The Mill on the Floss,* and driving around in a light wagon. Shaw noted his own "angelic mood" and liked not seeing "a single soul" other than his wife until the final day of the wedding trip.[5]

Then the worst happened. On May 6, the day Andrew took Secretary Chase to see the regiment, Hallowell telegraphed Shaw that he must return to camp because the governor had ordered the unit to depart on the twentieth. Additionally, after all the training, Hallowell had been ordered—against his wishes—to remain at Readville to organize a new black regiment, the Fifty-fifth. Shaw remained for two more melancholy days in Lenox, then returned to Boston on May 9. The next day the couple settled in again at Mrs. Crehore's, where they stayed until the regiment actually left Boston on May 28. In preparation for that spectacle, another ceremony was in order.[6]

 So Fine a Set of Men

WHILE ROBERT E. LEE planned his invasion of the North after his victory over Joe Hooker at Chancellorsville and while Ulysses Grant set siege to Vicksburg, on May 13 at the Camp Meigs training facility near Boston, Shaw pinned on the silver eagles denoting his promotion to colonel. For ninety days he had busily instructed his men, met with hundreds of visitors who came to see the North's first black regiment, and spent what spare time he had courting Annie Haggerty. Shaw had been successful in ensuring the fitness of his men, the approval of the visitors, and his marriage to Annie.

When the army's mustering officer had sworn the men into service, he admitted his beliefs that "it was a great joke to try to make soldiers of '*niggers*,'" but he told Shaw that he "had never mustered in so fine a set of men." Shaw did have one monumental task left—to prove that black men could fight and die like white men.[1]

Nearly two thousand members of Boston's black community and a vast group of others gathered at Readville on May 18 for the presentation of flags to the regiment. The four flags were the Stars and Stripes, the Massachusetts state flag, a white silk flag with the goddess of Liberty and the motto "Liberty, Loyalty, and Unity" incribed thereon, and a blue flag with a cross to symbolize Christ's mission. Women's "flag committees" presented each flag to the governor, who in turn handed them to Shaw. The themes of nation, state, manhood, home, Christianity, and higher law could hardly have been missed by the multitude. While many black Bostonians had initially discouraged their young men from joining the army, the community soon swung around to give encouragement, food, clothing, and sons. In all, 40 percent of black Bostonians of military age joined the Fifty-fourth or, later, the Fifty-fifth. Now they had come to Readville to see it all for themselves. Among them stood every prominent Boston abolitionist as well as Frederick Douglass and the members of Shaw's family, with the glaring exception of Shaw's mother, who was sick—for an unknown reason. Shaw formed the regiment into a hollow square around the speaker's platform.[2]

Governor Andrew presented the colors and left little doubt of the pressure that rested upon the men's shoulders for the vindication of a race, and of himself. Andrew recognized that his reputation as a man and a politician would "stand or fall" with the action of this regiment. The entire abolitionist community hoped with him that these men would not let them down. He talked of "character, the manly character, the zeal, the manly zeal, of the colored citizens" and pled with them "to strike a blow." Andrew put the burden of mankind upon them: "I know not . . . when, in all human history, to any given thousand men in arms there has been committed a work at once so proud, so precious, so full of hope and glory as the work committed to you." He told Shaw and the officers that he had a "confidence which knows no hesitation or doubt" that they would do their duty. After receiving the four flags and the governor's admonition that the unit must succeed, Shaw responded in a speech just six sentences long. He assured the crowd that his men knew "the importance of the undertaking." He hoped for "an opportunity to show that you have not made a mistake in intrusting the honor of the State to a colored regiment." The regiment entertained the crowd with a short drill before Shaw hosted a reception for the visitors at his headquarters. The colonel and his men had ten days to ponder the events of this day before they would leave the barracks of Massachusetts for the tents of South Carolina.[3]

The crowd lining the parade route in Boston on May 28 welcomed the steady breeze as they stood under a cloudless sky in near-summer weather. Many of the twenty thousand onlookers had purchased a remembrance of the day, a "Souvenir of the Massachusetts Fifty-Fourth," from which they read a quote from Byron: "Those who would be free, themselves must strike the blow." Finally, down the street came a large contingent of policemen leading mounted riders, two bands, a drum corps, and—what everyone had awaited—the men of the North's first black regiment. The sight of a thousand dark-skinned soldiers in arms marching behind "Old Glory" led one admiring reporter to gasp: "Can we believe our own eyes and ears? Is this Boston? Is it America?" This was the most spectacular abolitionist parade of the war and an expression of Bostonian moral dominance.[4]

Harriet Jacobs, a runaway slave whose *Incidents in the Life of a Slave Girl* (1861) illuminated the special horrors female slaves faced, was there to applaud the regiment. She recalled: "How my heart swelled with the thought that my poor oppressed race were to strike a blow for Freedom! Were at last allowed to help in breaking the chains." Shaw's mother looked upon her son, astride an ebony horse, and wondered aloud, in nearly the same words she would write to him the next day, "What have I done, that God has been so good to me!" One week later, she wrote her friend John Cairnes, a leading English abolitionist and author of *The Slave Power* (1862): "If I never see him again, I shall feel that he has not lived in vain." Amos Adams Lawrence of the black committee told his wife that nothing like this had been seen before, and at the head of it all came Shaw, "riding out front, as handsome as a picture. Everybody cheered him; the girls threw flowers at him." Another observer noted that this was "no parade" but a march led by a "boyish" commander with "only a simple air of determined devotion to duty." John Greenleaf Whittier remembered thinking that Shaw seemed as "beautiful and awful as an angel of God come down to lead the host of freedom to victory." A twenty-year-old William James later recalled that when he saw Shaw's sister Josephine and her fiancé, Charles Lowell, looking so "young and victorious," and with all the praise for Shaw, he was "gnawed by questions as to my own enlisting or not, [and] shrank back—they had not seen me—from being recognized." [5]

Of course, not everyone came to praise the Fifty-fourth. The Democrats of Boston's fashionable Somerset Club hissed the regiment as it passed their windows. Many of Boston's Irish felt that emancipation and the raising of black regiments threatened their tenuous position by enabling blacks to compete for the low-paying jobs they occupied. For weeks, the *Boston Pilot*, an organ of the Irish community, had alternately spread fear of black equality and ridiculed the idea that blacks would fight as men. In perhaps the most spirited attack, one critic wrote: "They are as fit to be soldiers of this country, as their abettors are to be its statesmen. One Southern regiment of white men would put twenty regiments of them to flight in half an hour. Twenty thousand negroes on the march would be smelled ten miles distant. No scouts need ever to be sent out to discover such warriors. There is not an American living that should not blush at the plan of making such a race the defenders of the national fame and power." Lieutenant Wilkie James remembered the "rankest sort" of prejudice and groans as the regiment wound through the streets of Boston. Overall, though, police and supporters far outnumbered the detractors; Shaw reported that he had "not seen such enthusiasm since the first troops left for the war."[6]

The regiment halted on Boston Common for an hour-long review and to hear speeches in its honor. Then Shaw dismissed the men to meet with well-wishers and to say goodbyes. Captain John Appleton remembered the "blessings, shouts & some tears— strangers clasped our hands and blessed us." Shaw met with his family for the last time, saying "good bye so stoically" to his wife, sisters, and mother, while going into a back room with Harry Russell for what he called "a regular girl's cry." After this short respite, Shaw ordered assembly. The men reformed, marched to Battery Wharf, and boarded the brand-new transport steamer *DeMolay*.[7]

Shaw had not yet informed the men of their destination, and rumors spread quickly. Once aboard the ship, Captain Appleton wrote his wife, "I tell you a secret that I think we are going to Newbern but maybe not." He had guessed wrong. The Fifty-fourth had orders to report to Major General David Hunter, commander of the Department of the South, headquartered at Hilton Head, South Carolina. Hunter requested Governor Andrew to send him the regiment and promised that he would put them to good service alongside white soldiers and with the units of freed slaves that had been organized under Thomas W. Higginson and James Montgomery. Hunter swore himself a friend of black troops, testified that "the prejudices of certain of our white soldiers and officers . . . are softening or fading out," and promised to use these "intelligent colored men from the North" to subdue the Rebels. Andrew had already been advocating this very arrangement with the secretary of war, once pleading with Stanton: "I pray you to send the 54th to So. Carolina, where, under Genl. Hunter, negro troops will be appreciated and allowed a place in . . . active war." By the middle of May, Stanton decided to grant Andrew's request.[8]

Frederick Douglass joined Massachusetts Adjutant General William Schouler and a few friends aboard the *DeMolay* as it made its way out of Boston Harbor. Once clear of the sound, Douglass bade farewell to his son Lewis, spoke with those he had recruited, and undoubtedly told others to do their duty. Shaw and the officers were already talking with a captain from Colonel Higginson's staff, who accompanied them to explain conditions and procedures under General Hunter. After a while, Douglass and the other guests climbed aboard another boat and returned to Boston. Schouler remembered all the hopes he felt as "the large vessel with its precious cargo" sailed into the night. So much rested on the conduct of this unit. The men, the officers, and Shaw knew the whole white and black world watched their every action. They had to be better than "good"; they had to be perfect.[9]

 South Carolina

THE SEA VOYAGE to Hilton Head took one week. It was unremarkable. Some men attempted to liven up the trip by drinking liquor smuggled aboard in direct violation of Shaw's orders. When the officers tried to enforce discipline by seizing the alcohol from intoxicated soldiers, some fighting—mostly pushing—erupted. In an ugly incident, one soldier stabbed another in the face with a bayonet. In another, Shaw ordered a *DeMolay* crewman lashed to the ship's rigging for stealing from a soldier. Dr. Stone treated

seven men for illness and many more for seasickness. The one fa-
tality was Major Hallowell's horse, whose burial the men made
into a ceremony, consigning the body to the sea. Mostly, the voyage
offered little entertainment. The men talked of loved ones left behind, wondered if and when they would get a chance to fight, and
sang away the monotony. On the fifth day out, they steamed past
Charleston, saw the blockading fleet and the top of Fort Sumter,
and were amazed at the fury of a thunderstorm. Everyone quickly
tired of water and sky and close quarters and longed to stand again
on dry land.[1]

Shaw contemplated the events of the past three months, focus-
ing on the raising of the regiment and his courtship and marriage.
As the steamer neared Cape Hatteras, he wrote proudly to Annie,
telling her, "The more I think of the passage of the Fifty-fourth
through Boston, the more wonderful it seems to me. Just remember our own doubts and fears, and other people's sneering and pity-
ing remarks, when we began last winter, and then look at the perfect triumph of last Thursday." Exhilarated by the praise and
changed by the conduct of his men, Shaw continued, "Truly, I
ought to be thankful for all my happiness, and my success in life
so far; and if the raising of coloured troops prove such a benefit to
the country, and to the blacks . . . I shall thank God a thousand
times that I was led to take my share in it."[2]

The *DeMolay* docked at Hilton Head on June 3. Shaw disembarked and reported directly to General Hunter, who formally inspected the regiment, found it "excellent," and ordered it to Port
Royal Island, where Col. W. W. Davis would assign a campground.
As the ship steamed upriver twelve miles to Beaufort, Shaw and
his men saw, most of them for the first time, scenes of the Old
South. Captain Appleton described the sights of "mansions and the
long rows of Negro houses, here and there, also groups of Red and
yellow dressed mammys. . . . We ran from side to side of the ship
to see the different plantations." The Fifty-fourth arrived at Beau-

fort to great fanfare as several bands and hundreds of onlookers celebrated the arrival of the already-famous regiment from the North. There, immediately, the men met another group of black soldiers, the contraband regiment of Colonel James Montgomery. The Second South Carolina, with Harriet Tubman acting as scout, had just returned from its raid up the Combahee River, where it burned property and transported 725 slaves to freedom. Burgeoning with bodies of the always free, recently freed, and less-than-a-day-freed men and women, Beaufort had proportionatey more abolitionists than any city in the world at that time. The men and officers of the two black regiments no doubt looked upon each other with curiosity and wondered about their differences. After remaining in cramped quarters aboard the steamer for one more night, the Fifty-fourth happily streamed single file down the gangplank to set up camp in what had been an old cottonfield. With no Rebel army nearby, the only enemies were the insects and snakes the men found everywhere. At least one rattlesnake died to make room for the tents. Appleton complained to his wife that "sand flies, midges, mosquitoes, stinging ants, [and] little red ticks, . . . leave very little of us."[3]

Shaw wrote to Governor Andrew informing him of the arrival in South Carolina. He mentioned Montgomery and, even though he had never seen the colonel in action, derided his "Indian style of fighting." Shaw hoped for the same scale of battles—and glory—he had grown used to in the Second Massachusetts, complaining, "Bushwacking seems pretty small potatoes." In fact, Montgomery was a specialist at raiding, something he had learned in Kansas, when as mentor to—then student of—John Brown, he spread fire and brimstone among the proslavery settlers. Brown sometimes stayed in Montgomery's house, cooperated with him on dashes into Missouri, and called him "a lover of freedom." Shaw would have much to say later about Montgomery's methods. Still worrying over what others thought and feeling protective and insecure, Shaw was relieved that most of the officers at Beaufort treated him well, even though many of them seemed "rather coppery."[4]

On the day the regiment went into camp, Shaw met Colonel Thomas Wentworth Higginson, the only prominent New England abolitionist to command black troops during the war, and a different sort of soldier from Montgomery. Higginson and Montgomery had known each other before the war, when they were allies in the Kansas struggle, but they didn't agree on methods. Analyzing the difference between them, historian Dudley T. Cornish concluded that Higginson had been brought up, and limited, by Harvard notions of fairness, while Montgomery learned from experience. Cornish noted that "Higginson the romantic, had raised money to send Sharp's rifles to Kansas in the fifties. Montgomery, the realist, had used them."[5]

Higginson manned his regiment, the First South Carolina Volunteers, with exslaves from the nearby plantations and became the most experienced officer in any black regiment. Shaw described him as "one who put his whole soul into his work." Impressed with "his open-heartedness & purity of character," Shaw sought his insight into the fighting ability of the recruits. For Higginson's part, he liked that Shaw "asked only sensible questions" about the performance of black troops and declared the "matter of courage to be settled." Shaw still wondered if his men would stand well when the musketry crackled, and he suggested to Higginson that perhaps it would be good to put the soldiers "between two fires" so that battle-proven white men at their backs would "present equal danger in either direction" and prevent them from running in the face of the enemy. While he knew that white rookies commonly ran during their first fight, Shaw feared that if his men fled, Northern whites would seize on the example to "confirm" black inferiority and to persuade the government to withdraw its black regiments. At the least, any cowardice by the Fifty-fourth would create trouble with and suspicion among white units, who would be afraid to fight beside them. More than that, though, Shaw still struggled with his own racism and would not exorcise fully his belief in inferiority until his men proved themselves in front of the Confederate army.[6]

Two days later, Hunter ordered the regiment to Hilton Head and then to Saint Simons Island, Georgia, seventy-five miles to the south, to rendezvous with Montgomery's regiment, which had preceded it. The Fifty-fourth arrived at Saint Simons at six o'clock on the morning of June 9, after a stormy trip over rough seas. John Appleton noted their proximity to Jekyll Island, where in 1858 Charles Lamar's infamous ship *Wanderer* unloaded a cargo of 409 Africans. Since the U.S. Constitution specifically prohibited the importation of slaves after 1808, authorities had seized the ship and prosecuted Lamar. Even though Lamar escaped conviction, his action increased sectional tension. Appleton confidently remarked, "I think no more will be landed there for some time." Montgomery too knew of Lamar's action, and it kindled in him a resolve to make good on his oath that slaveholders must suffer for their sins against humanity.[7]

26 Burning Georgia

DURING HIS THIRD MONTH at war, Shaw, in Virginia, had visited the site of John Brown's 1859 raid on Harper's Ferry and his jail cell in Charlestown. Now in his third year of war, Shaw, in South Carolina, became entranced by James Montgomery, who had been Brown's compatriot in the days when Kansas bled. On June 5 he informed his father that "Montgomery is a good man to begin under"; the next day he wrote his mother that "the bush-whacker Montgomery is a strange compound . . . & looks as if he had quite a taste for hanging people & throat-cutting whenever a suitable subject offers." Despite this early ambivalence, Shaw rapidly came to admire Montgomery's past work, dedication to abolition, attractive looks, and adherence to discipline.[1]

In the morning of June 9, Shaw established his Saint Simons headquarters in "Rosemount"—the abandoned plantation house of James Gould—and put his men into what he described as "a very nice camping-ground" nearby. In the early afternoon, he sat down to write to Annie, telling her, "You would be enchanted with the scenery here; the foliage is wonderfully thick, and the trees covered with hanging moss, making beautiful avenues." Before he could finish his letter, Montgomery interrupted him with an invitation to participate in a raid. Hurriedly accepting, and leaving behind a camp guard, it took Shaw only thirty minutes to board his men onto transports to join the expedition. He had been eager to get into action and grasped this chance for it.[2]

As the superior officer, Montgomery directed the strike force of three transports and one gunboat on an overnight excursion up the Altamaha River to Darien, a seaport town that had been Georgia's second leading port. Antebellum Darien actively engaged in supplying cotton, rice, turpentine, and timber to the world market; and although that commercial activity had been almost completely shut down by the North's naval blockade, Montgomery claimed that the town was still a rendezvous point for blockade runners. At the time Montgomery and Shaw arrived, the townspeople had removed themselves and their slaves further inland for safer haven. The four-boat expeditionary force waited for the flood tide before proceeding through the sea marsh. As Shaw described it, "We wound in and out through the creeks, twisting and turning continually, often heading in directly the opposite direction from that which we intended to go, and often running aground."[3]

Montgomery had his artillery throw "several shells among the plantation[s] . . . in a very brutal way" as they approached the "beautiful little town." After a noontime shelling of the town just before docking, the men landed to no opposition. Shaw followed Montgomery's example, assembled his men in the streets, then detailed them to gather supplies. One officer recalled Shaw's order: "Captain Appleton, take twenty men from the right of your company, break into the houses on this street, take out anything that can be made useful in camp." The men did as they were told and "began to come in by twos, threes, and dozens, loaded with every species and all sorts and quantities of furniture, stores, trinkets, etc. . . . We had sofas, tables, pianos, chairs, mirrors, carpets, beds." One soldier, thinking of his stomach instead of his back, had "a brace of chickens in one hand, and in the other hand a rope with a cow attached." Lieutenant James Grace of the New Bedford company described the loot to General Peirce at Readville: "I wish you could see my tent all furnished with rosewood and black walnut furniture, looking glasses, pictures, some very fine ones. Some of our officers got very nice carpets." [4]

While participating willingly in the plunder, Shaw was indignant when Montgomery turned to him with his "sweet smile" and said in a very low tone, "I shall burn this town." Thinking the action unjustified and disgraceful, Shaw could have assented to it only if they had met Rebel resistance. A year earlier, in Virginia, the Second Massachusetts set fire to Winchester during their retreat. That time, an angry Shaw reported, "I hope the town will be destroyed when we go back there. We had time to burn part of it while the fight was going on." This time, he thought the action a "dirty piece of business" which brought "dishonour." He feared that such "wanton destruction" would bring negative publicity to black soldiering. In camp he had been careful to enforce strict discipline, now his efforts would go for naught if this action hurt public opinion, which was far from decided about black soldiers. Charles Lowell wrote Josephine that Shaw "must be peculiarly disturbed" about what had happened. Lowell feared that "instead of improving the negro character and educating him for a civilized independence, we are re-developing all his savage instincts." Writing the War Department to complain against using blacks to destroy property, Lowell warned that if this continued, "no first-rate officers" would join black regiments. He explained that the end result would not be "an army of disciplined blacks, . . . [but] a horde of savages." Obviously, if Lowell ascribed to the argument of latent violence within black bodies, others, less committed to the end of slavery, would see the worst.[5]

North and South, newspapers carried the story. Confederate papers and Northern detractors of black troops naturally berated the action. An article in the *Savannah News* was widely reprinted. Among other epithets, that paper called the Fifty-fourth "accursed Yankee vandals," "wretches," and "cowardly Yankee negro thieves." In a book found in Darien, Private Stewart Woods, a twenty-seven-year-old laborer from Carlisle, Pennsylvania, had written his name, his regiment, and the names of his officers, including Shaw. Because of that graffito, which was actually a message of pride from a free-black soldier to black and white Southern readers, many began to blame Shaw for torching civilian property. The men of the Fifty-fourth knew that the opposition press objected to the raid by "nigger guerillas" upon Darien. The raid and the negative response put even more pressure on the men and Shaw to redeem themselves at the earliest opportunity.[6]

Montgomery always defended the burning of private homes as a way to make Southerners "feel that this was a real war." Because of the hostility against black soldiers, Montgomery also felt "outlawed, and therefore not bound by the rules of regular warfare." A religious man with a bit of the Calvinist belief that "nothing happens by chance," he told Shaw that slaveowners "must be swept away by the hand of God, like the Jews of old." He had even set the last buildings afire with his own hand. All this was too much for Shaw, who shared Higginson's Harvard notions of fair play and loathed the idea of burning private homes that might be occupied by innocent women and children. Shaw often referred to the Darien affair as a "barbarous sort of warfare," "abominable," and as lacking of any "pluck or courage."[7]

Others rallied to defend the act. Frederick Douglass insisted that the Confederate Congress and President Jefferson Davis must be made to understand that their unjust actions declaring white officers be put to death and black soldiers to be sold into slavery would not be tolerated. Douglass said if burnings were necessary to force the Rebels to adhere to "rules of civilized warfare" then let the torch be applied. The *Boston Commonwealth* called the action "divine justice" against "those who have so long traded in human bodies and souls" and deemed it retaliation for what Confederate navy commerce raiders—such as Raphael Semmes's *Alabama*—were doing to Union shipping. At the same time, the *Commonwealth* warned that this hurt the Fifty-fourth, which had won "prestige" that would soon be "wasted." Shaw could agree with this paper's admonition that blacks already suffered from a "vast accumulation of undeserved odium" and must therefore "be employed only in the strictest duties of war." White soldiers could set fires with impunity; black soldiers would fan the flames of racial hatred if they struck a single spark. Shaw knew this and resented Montgomery for casting a shadow over his honor and his men's reputation. He reported to Governor Andrew that the raid "disgusted" him, and claimed his men "superior" to the contraband regiments and worthy of better service.[8]

Shaw also wrote a letter to Hunter's adjutant, Lieutenant Colonel Charles Halpine, and complained about the "barbarous" burning of the town. Montgomery had told Shaw that he had his orders from Hunter, and Shaw wanted to know if Hunter had indeed issued such instructions. Shaw said that if Hunter deemed future actions necessary, he would do it, but he did not like it. As it turned out, Montgomery had been acting on Hunter's orders.

Shaw's hope for a change in policy came true, for a short while. Lincoln too had been reading the papers and felt aggrieved over Hunter's scorched-earth policy. Lincoln knew his political life marched with the public's opinion of black troops, so he replaced Hunter with a less vindictive general.[9]

Sometime during all this, Shaw gained a "feeling of great respect" for Montgomery. He described him as a man "quiet, gentlemanly, full of determination, . . . [whose] perfect calmness at all times is very impressive." Shaw's admiration undoubtedly came from the long talks the two had around the headquarters buildings at night and from listening to the high opinion superior officers offered. Montgomery told him he believed "the South must be devasted with fire & sword" partly because he had come "to hate every enemy of liberty." Shaw liked Montgomery's spirit, and told Charles Lowell that "Montgomery, who seems the only active man in this Department, is enormously energetic, and devoted to the cause." Shaw continued the flattery: "He is very prompt & active, never lying idle, if he can help it, for more than three days at a time. When delayed and disappointed, he is wonderfully patient & calm. . . . I never met a man who impressed me as being more conscientious." Physically too, Montgomery had gripped Shaw with "his eye (which bye the bye, is very extraordinary) . . . that very queer roll or glare in his eye—and a contraction of the eyebrows every now & then, which gives him rather a fierce expression." Shaw later admitted the obvious to his mother: "He is very attractive to me, and indeed I have taken a great fancy to him." [10]

On Saint Simons after the Darien raid, Shaw assured his men that they would have better duty and told them they must be ready to prove their detractors wrong. Shaw's old stereotypes of blacks as savages resurfaced as he thought about what had transpired in Darien. Fighting against his racism while determining to keep his men in line, Shaw ordered that any soldier who discharged his rifle without supervision or who became a "nuisance" would be "severely punished." He warned that if the men slept on duty or deserted, he would have them shot. Initially, because of the heat, the regiment drilled four hours a day, from five to seven in the morning and from four to six every afternoon. Later, to keep the men busy, or perhaps unhappy with what he saw or feared, Shaw ordered an extra drill from eight to ten. Company sergeants met daily to recite lessons and tactics. Every day, Shaw inspected his men and equipment. After one unsatisfactory review, Shaw chastised five of the ten companies for the unpolished condition of their rifles. Every evening before dinner, Shaw reviewed the regiment in a formal dress parade. He enforced taps at 9:30 P.M. There is no evidence to support a conjecture that soldiers in the regiment now behaved differently than they had at Readville or that participation with the contraband regiment had diminished their soldierly bearing. Fearing a loss of discipline, Shaw made his men pay for his insecurity with increased drill.[11]

Shaw pined for a standup battle instead of raids or sequestration from white troops and main arenas of battle. He soon got his wish, when the regiment returned to Hilton Head on June 25 to support the coming assault upon Charleston. Shaw settled the men into camp on Saint Helena Island and waited for action. During this period Shaw often reevaluated Colonel Montgomery, a man he greatly respected but did not understand. Shaw admired Montgomery's dedication and envied his clear vision of vengeance and mission. Besides the Darien raid, Shaw watched Montgomery shoot a man for disorderly conduct and execute a soldier for desertion. Undoubtedly, Shaw liked Montgomery for his adherence to discipline. But Shaw believed that Montgomery's troops were inferior to his own because they were made up of contrabands from the plantations who had "never had the pluck to run away" before the war started. Shaw's letters reveal this lack of vision and his belief that Southern blacks were "perfectly childlike . . . no more

responsible for their actions than so many puppies." He also wrote
of the freed people as having "utter ignorance, and innocence of
evil." Shaw admired Montgomery for leading troops made up of
exslaves, but he believed his Northern men were better; certainly,
his disdain for the South affected his analysis. Additionally, as an
extension of abolitionist thought that freedom uplifted and made
better men, Shaw had to believe his men were better soldiers because of their prewar experiences in the North. Constantly doubt-
ing his own abilities and worried about his men, he sought comparisons to deal with his insecurity.[12]

27 Fanny Kemble and Charlotte Forten

SHAW ADMITTED THAT he sometimes thought too much, "until
I am pretty *home*-sick." He dreamed of domestic bliss, wishfully
asking Annie, "Shall we ever have a home of our own, do you
suppose?" While reaffirming his commitment to duty, he admitted, "I can't help looking forward to that time, though I should
not." For a young man, newly married, far from home, and still
uncertain of his choice to leave his beloved Second Massachusetts
for an untested regiment, loneliness and homesickness are under-
standable responses. He hoped to rejoin Annie sometime in the
winter but warned her, "Don't set your heart upon it." Adding to
his loneliness was the severe disruption in mail delivery. Shaw had
grown accustomed to the lifeline to home brought in the words of
letters and love letters. Now, in South Carolina and Georgia, mail
came erratically, and Shaw, feeling neglected—even though the
volume of letters being written to him never diminished—often
complained bitterly about being forgotten. At one point he told
his mother that he was "so sorry & provoked at getting no word

from Annie, that I didn't know what to do." He sought pleasure where he could find it. Certainly, everything was not hardship and want.[1]

Wilkie James called the island "a perfect paradise . . . with its wealth of tropical beauty. . . . The live oak and the magnolia, the orange, the lemon and the palmetto, the citron, the fig-tree and the yellow jessamine attained apparent perfection." Mission walls built under the supervision of Spanish priests and the tabby construction of oyster shells, lime, and beach sand of James Oglethorpe's Fort Frederica whispered the romantic military history of the island to a new generation of soldiers. Appleton concentrated his descriptions on the two alligators that were killed in camp and the daily sightings of rattlesnakes everywhere. The city-boy Shaw was shocked by the "St. Simons River, full of alligators . . . mak[ing] such a noise at night, that I, at first, thought it was a vessel blowing off steam." Gooding admitted, "To tell the honest truth, our boys out on picket look sharper for snakes than they do for rebels." The men ate well on the cattle deserted by a Rebel owner and on turtle eggs dug from the beach. They bathed in seawater and rinsed in the rains that swept the island. Some soldiers spruced up their tents with furniture pulled from Darien mansions and spent the bulk of each day searching for shade in which to read and think of home.[2]

Shaw situated himself in the absent owner's house and added to its furnishings with accent pieces from Darien. He spent his spare time writing letters and studying manuals on military tactics. Perhaps the increased drill he put the men through was more for his preparation than theirs; not a captain obeying orders, he was a colonel giving them.

Besides attending to the regiment, Shaw basked in the loveliness of the island and took time to visit some of the plantations he had heard Fanny Kemble describe during the long-ago summer in Sor-

rento. As it turned out, Kemble's *Journal of a Residence on a Georgian Plantation*, published in May 1863, allowed abolitionists to
read about what Shaw was seeing firsthand. The plantation homes
of T. Butler King, James E. Couper, and Pierce Butler provided a
contrast to the slave cabins that stood nearby, and Shaw wrote with
a tourist's excitement, tempered by the realization that the glory
of his surroundings rested on the foundations of slavery. Shaw was
drawn to Butler's plantation, where he talked with some of the old
slaves still in residence, having been left over from the 1859 sale
of 429 slaves—the largest single sale of human beings in American history. They told him that even though Butler "had sold their
sons & daughters they said he was a good Marst'r." Many of them
fondly recalled Fanny Kemble and wanted Shaw to remember
them to her if he saw her again. Shaw described the freed people
as "faithful creatures" and affirmed his antislavery convictions that
every abandoned plantation "is a harbinger of freedom to the
slaves." Still, Shaw obviously did not think of all blacks as equal.[5]

He missed his mother and his wife but managed to find female
companionship in the Northern schoolteachers who came to Port
Royal to teach those who had been newly freed. At first glance,
Shaw thought the "Northern ladies here are a fearful crowd—
ungrammatical and nasal"; but, with limited choices, he soon
sought them out. On July 2 he rode five miles across a shell road
to take tea at a nearby plantation house where teachers lived.
There he met and enjoyed socializing with twenty-six-year-old
Charlotte Forten of Philadelphia, the only African American mis-
sionary teaching on Saint Helena. He described her as "a quad-
roon . . . quite pretty, remarkably well educated, and a very inter-
esting woman." With a similar racial and class-based gaze, Lydia
Maria Child once described Forten as "queenly enough for a
model of Cleopatra." Forten came from a prominent family of abolitionists with wide social connections—her uncle James Purvis

headed the American Anti-Slavery Society in 1863. She had been educated in an integrated school in Salem, Massachusetts, before volunteering to go to Beaufort in October 1862.[4]

Shaw spent nearly a week in her company, often seeing her day and night. His four-day letter to his mother dated July 3–6 indicated his infatuation for the one he called "decidedly the belle here." All the officers were after her. Forten was equally taken with Shaw and, after what she called "a pleasant talk on the moonlit piazza," wrote that she was "perfectly charmed" by "one of the most delightful persons I have ever met." She found him tender with "something girlish about him, and yet I never saw anyone more manly. To me he seems a perfectly lovable person."[5]

On July 4 they spent the Independence Day celebration together, gathered with a few thousand others in the churchyard of the Baptist church seven miles from camp. The weather cooperated perfectly, the "gay dresses of the women made the sight very brilliant," and the crowd assembled "under some magnificent old oaks, covered with the long, hanging, grey moss." Shaw was moved by the mass of African American voices when "a little black boy read the Declaration of Independence, and then, they all sang some of our hymns." After hearing former slaves sing their own songs, unheard before by Shaw, Forten promised him she would write down the words so he could send them to his mother. Further knowing his mother's inclinations, Shaw reported all the news to her, and asked, "Can you imagine anything more wonderful than a coloured-Abolitionist meeting on a South Carolina plantation? Here were collected all the freed slaves on this Island listening to the most ultra abolition speeches . . . while two years ago, their masters were still here, the lords of the soil & of them." Citing the "most extraordinary change" since then, Shaw became more religious than ever before, asserting that "God isn't very far off."[6]

Shaw and Forten visited again the next day, and the next, as Forten again confessed to her journal of being "more than ever

charmed with the noble little Col. What purity, what nobleness of
soul, what exquisite gentleness in that beautiful face! As I look at
it I think 'The bravest are the tenderest.'" Shaw and a few other
officers had invited her and "two other ladies to tea" and entertained them with "some singing from the men." That night both
of them wrote about each other, Shaw to his mother, Forten in her
journal. Shaw compared the evening with the pleasant ones he
had at Readville with Annie. Forten wrote: "Yesterday . . . lean-
ing against our carriage and speaking of mother, so lovingly, so
tenderly. He said he wished she c'ld be there. . . . I do think he
is a wonderfully lovable person." Then, writing within her own
passion—and maybe his—she dreamily confided, "To-night, he
helped me on my horse, and after carefully arranging the folds of
my riding skirt, said, so kindly, 'Goodbye. If I don't see you again
down here I hope to see you at our house.' But I hope I shall have
the pleasure of seeing him many times even down here."[7]

Obviously, Forten and Shaw were strongly taken with each
other. For Shaw, being so far from home and questioning himself
and his men, this intelligent, admiring, desirable woman gave him
impossibly much when he had gotten accustomed to so much less.
No one can be certain of what intimacies may or may not have
been shared between the two. It is clear that before their relationship could develop further, the war intervened.

28 They Fought like Heroes

EVEN WHILE HE socialized with Charlotte Forten and others,
Shaw fretted over being left behind when the other troops, white
troops, moved to support the activities around Charleston. His men
were being used primarily for "loading and discharging vessels."
On July 6 he complained to General George C. Strong, the brigade

commander in charge of the Fifty-fourth and a man sympathetic to the need for blacks to fight alongside whites. Shaw expressed his disappointment at not being part of the campaign. He flattered Strong and requested "better service than mere guerilla warfare." Shaw understood that to lift the popular opinion of black troops it was paramount "that the colored soldiers should be associated as much as possible with the white troops, in order that they may have other witnesses besides their own officers to what they are capable of doing." Strong liked Shaw, agreed with him, and promised to honor the request to get him into the actual assault upon Charleston, if possible. For the time being, however, the Fifty-fourth had a different assignment.[1]

On July 8 the regiment readied for transport to James Island. The men were excited. After their segregated employment on raids, perhaps they were finally going to be integrated in battle with white regiments. Maybe they would even get a chance to use the Enfields they had fired only in target practice. With thoughts of Darien and the renewed criticism of black troops that came with the burning there, the men wanted more than ever to prove that they could fight like white men. Some were upset that they would have to stay behind as camp guards and for other detail duty. Of those going toward the front, many worried whether they could stand up to the test of battle. They believed they could, and their discipline and training helped them steady themselves for a fight to the finish; but they were afraid nonetheless.

The officers also reflected the tension of the moment. A week before, there had been an awful rumor that the government had decided to arm black troops with pikes instead of rifles. Some of the officers and men were angry and more than a few talked of quitting if that happened. Shaw wrote home that "pikes against Minie balls is not fair play—especially in the hands of negroes whose great pride lies in being a soldier like white men." He worried that such a move would "be the ruin of all spirit & courage" and added, in another missive, "They might as well go back eighteen centuries as three, and give us bows and arrows." Although John Brown had wanted to distribute pikes during his crusade, Shaw had seen too many modern battles to support that kind of insanity. But Captain Appleton coolly told the officers: "I came out to prove that colored men could fight and I would go into action armed with pickaxes if ordered." His bravado noted, the rumor passed, and everyone kept a rifle. With relief and the hope to begin firing the guns into the enemy, Shaw supervised the loading of the seven companies—about seven hundred men—aboard two transport ships bound for James Island.[2]

Shipboard, another issue dominated conversation. The government had ordered that its black men in arms be paid ten dollars a month—the pay for laborers—instead of the thirteen dollars per month that white soldiers received. Additionally, their pay would be docked three dollars per month for clothing expenses instead of being supplemented by the same amount, as was the practice for white soldiers. The men, who were already suffering for a want of an initial paycheck, were hurt by this racial decision that put less of a premium on black lives and soldiering ability than it did on white ones. Promises had been made when the Fifty-fourth was organized that recruits would get equal pay for equal work. The earliest recruiting poster tacked up in Boston announced not only a bounty of one hundred dollars and state aid to families, but also promised "Pay, $13 a Month!" An angry Shaw thought it best "to refuse to allow them to be paid" and held that if the government kept to this insanity, his men should "be mustered out of service, as they were enlisted on the understanding that they were to be on the same footing as other Mass. Vols." After he wrote to Governor Andrew of this "great piece of injustice," Andrew supported the regiment with letters to Lincoln and Stanton. From inside the unit, most of the men firmly refused to accept any pay cut. Corporal James Gooding wrote directly to Lincoln and asked,

"Now the main question is, Are we *soldiers*, or are we *Labourers?*" Lincoln never answered the letter. The men would have to refuse pay until September 29, 1864, when Congress finally equalized pay. Undoubtedly, only the fighting that came after the regiment steamed toward James Island—and the later charge against Fort Wagner—swayed Congress to do the right thing.[3]

General Quincy A. Gillmore, who had replaced Hunter as commander of the Department of the South, was famous as the artillerist who had used a few well-placed shots to force the surrender of powerful Fort Pulaski on Tybee Island near Savannah. Gillmore now planned to reduce the forts and batteries that protected Charleston Harbor, to seize Fort Sumter, and to conquer the city where the rebellion began. Troops on James Island would divert attention from the real assault against Morris Island's Fort Wagner, which protected the guns defending the harbor at Cummings Point. Lincoln and his generals had hoped that Charleston could be taken by water. On April 7, 1863, Admiral Samuel du Pont led nine ironclads into the harbor and tried to destroy Fort Sumter. When he withdrew, five monitors were disabled, as Confederate cannon fired 2,209 shells against 154 thrown by du Pont's fleet. New plans combined a naval operation with a land assault against the defenses ringing the harbor. The most formidable line was Fort Wagner, which guarded one of the Confederate's key artillery positions protecting Charleston Harbor. On July 11, after a heavy bombardment of Wagner, Gillmore sent his infantry in a frontal assault, only to be repulsed with heavy losses. That same afternoon, after waiting aboard ship at anchor for two days, the Fifty-fourth landed on James Island. Shaw thought that Gillmore would probably begin siege operations against Wagner; but the general was still hoping for a quicker solution.[4]

While Gillmore made plans to renew the attack, Shaw put his men into camp. He enjoyed the sunset over the river and "from a housetop saw Fort Sumter, our Monitors, and the spires of Charleston." He had been wondering about his friends—especially Charles Morse—in his beloved Second Massachusetts and got the news that Lee had been defeated at Gettysburg and that Vicksburg had capitulated. A newspaper casualty list saddened him with the news of the death of his Harvard classmate and Second Massachusetts compatriot Charles Mudge at Gettysburg. Shaw told Annie that "every one must expect to lose their friends and relatives, and consider themselves as particularly favoured by Providence if they do not." He longed for the glory days of his past and admitted, "As regards my own pleasure, I had rather have that place [in the Second Massachusetts] than any other in the army." He thought about "the excitement there must be through the North" but could "not believe the end is coming yet." As a sideshow to the main action against Charleston, Shaw hoped for but did not expect any action on James Island. At least his pickets were on duty beside white soldiers from other regiments, and that was a beginning, even if they were being exploited as camp guards. Captain Cabot Russel informed his father that "the men behave exceedingly well on picket, of which we have been having a large dose." Still, Russel wrote that "their spirits are super."[5]

Then unexpectedly, at dawn on July 16, a 900-man Confederate force screamed the Rebel yell and slammed into the pickets. Russel's company and two others—about 250 men of the Fifty-fourth—quickly rallied and stubbornly held their ground in good order under the heavy assault. Forced to retreat, the regiment fought a delaying action that prevented the enemy from routing it and a white regiment, the Tenth Connecticut. Still, the Confederates pushed them back until the Union soldiers found protection under the artillery of their gunboats. They prepared for a last stand that never came. Just as suddenly as the attack began, it ended.[6]

Receiving praise from General Gillmore and from white soldiers, Shaw exulted that "to-day wipes out the remembrance of the Darien affair." Shaw was thrilled when General Alfred H. Terry, in charge of the Union division on James Island, congratulated him, saying that the best-disciplined white regiments could have done no better. Shaw's men had fought well in coordination with white soldiers against white Confederates. He had wanted to prove that black men could fight, and they had shown their valor. Captain Russel, whose life was saved by Private Preston Williams, explained simply: "My men did nobly." Captain Appleton wrote that the men's "stubborn courage filled the officers with joy." The soldiers of the Tenth Connecticut Infantry, camped next to the Fifty-fourth, were convinced by what they saw. One of them wrote his wife: "But for the bravery of . . . the Massachusetts Fifty-fourth (colored), our whole regiment would have been captured." He concluded with the greatest praise available: "They fought like heroes." Hearing such a response to black soldiers, Captain Appleton remembered, "These first praises of white men made the dusky cheeks burn." [7]

Shaw called the fight "a fortunate day . . . for me and for us all, excepting some poor fellows who were killed and wounded." He seemed to think the sacrifice of fourteen killed, eighteen wounded, and thirteen missing a small price to pay for the proof and praises he received. In his defense, the casualties were small compared with what he had seen in Virginia. He recognized the fight for what it was: "a fine thing for the coloured troops." With an ear to the Confederate promise to give no quarter to black Union prisoners, he reported conflicting rumors that "some prisoners were shot" and that "the Rebels treated them very kindly." In fact, a few prisoners may have been killed because of skin color; but there is little to substantiate a general slaughter anything close to that ordered by Nathan Bedford Forrest at Fort Pillow in 1864. Shaw wanted to send along another letter full of details of the battle, but he would never have the time to write it. To save his outnumbered troops on

James Island against further attack and to bolster his forces on Morris Island for another assault against Fort Wagner, Gillmore ordered Terry's division to Morris Island.[8]

29 The Grand Opportunity

WITHDRAWING AT 9:30 P.M., just a few hours after the battle on July 16, the Fifty-fourth made a difficult night march through the mud flats between James and Cole Islands. Engineers laid wooden planks, and the men marched single file over them for nearly eight hours. A moonless night and a relentless thunderstorm with lightning flashing all around made things worse, as the planks got slippery and men fell into the marsh. Whole companies stood — with nowhere to sit — in the hard rain as long minutes passed in extricating humans from the hydraulic grip of coastal quicksand. The alligators and sea grass only increased the misery. Shaw said he never had such "an extraordinary walk." Across Cole Island, at dawn, the regiment reached its transport rendezvous point exhausted, dirty, famished, and parched. "The sun and sand are dazzling and roasting us," Shaw wrote. As for the lack of food, "It seems like old times in the army of the Potomac." No change of clothes was available for either the colonel or his men and they ate the last of the "hard-bread and salt junk" stashed away in their pockets and packs. The men slept all day on the beach, searched for shelter from the sun, and watched for the steamers that would take them closer to Gillmore.[1]

At an hour before midnight on July 17, the regiment boarded the transport *General Hunter.* The loading took five hours and was delayed by another thunderstorm. Finally, the steamer ferried them to Follys Island, which they marched up, waited on the beach, looked upon the distant Forts Sumter and Wagner, then boarded another transport to cross the five-hundred-yard-wide inlet to Morris Island. They could hear the firing and concussions of shells bursting as Gillmore unleashed the entirety of his artillery upon the Confederate Fort Wagner. While his men made the two-hour march up Morris Island, Shaw rode ahead and reported to General Strong's headquarters.[2]

Strong told Shaw that Gillmore had ordered another infantry assault upon Wagner later that evening. Strong's brigade would lead. He probably did not tell Shaw of General Truman Seymour's comment to Gillmore when the attack plan had been formulated: "Well I guess we will let Strong put those d——d negroes from Massachusetts in the advance, we may as well get rid of them, one time as another." Federal artillery, monitors, and floating batteries had been pumping shells into Wagner since noon. The fort's defenders must be dead, wounded, or demoralized. It was almost six in the evening. The attack would come at dusk—a mere two hours away. Shaw and his men looked "worn and weary." Strong had become friends with Shaw in the tents at Saint Helena and admired the soft-spoken young man with the heavy load to bear. He told Shaw that the James Island fight gave the regiment credibility. Strong offered Shaw what Wilkie James later called "the grand chance . . . the one chance which above all others seemed essential!" Strong held out "opportunity." He asked Shaw if he wanted the Fifty-fourth to lead the charge. Shaw could have declined. His men were more than a little tired and hungry. But Shaw knew that the key to Charleston lay at the end of the beach. If black men could storm the fort and open the door to the birthplace of the rebellion, the symbolism would be enormous. His duty was never clearer. Since that day at Readville, when the first black civilian put on a soldier's uniform and Shaw began to instruct a regiment, this had been the goal. The chance for the sons of slaves to show that they would fight and thus to vindicate those who supported them suddenly reached out its hand to Shaw. His answer was yes.[3]

Even while Shaw believed that he would die in the battle forth-coming, he overcame that fear to do his duty. He never felt com-fortable in the Fifty-fourth and always considered himself a part of the Second. Maybe the responsibility was too much. Colonel Higginson remembered that when he met Shaw at Beaufort, Shaw had a "watchful anxiety in his look." Higginson believed that Shaw felt the destiny of a race upon his shoulders. On July 13 Shaw had written Annie that he would probably be a major in the Sec-ond had he stayed: "As regards my own pleasure, I had rather have that place than any other in the army." Of course, that admission came after news of more friends killed, this time at Gettysburg. Also, the fight on James Island had not yet happened. Shaw had committed himself to the Fifty-fourth, but he missed the days when he had close friends around him and less on the line. On July 15 Shaw confided to Hallowell his fear of dying and said that if a fight came, "I trust God will give me strength to do my duty." Just hours before saying yes to Strong, a melancholy Shaw sat on the transport between Folly and Morris Island and told Hallowell, "If I could only live a few weeks longer with my wife, and be at home a little while, I might die happy, but it cannot be. I do not believe I will live through our next fight." Still, Shaw hid his fear from the other officers and men.[4]

30 Fort Wagner

SHAW LED HIS MEN to the front, through or past the thirteen white regiments that would support the Fifty-fourth in the assault. Many white soldiers cheered the men they had come to respect. Many others believed, and some hoped, that black soldiers would not stand the test of manhood. At six hundred yards from the fort, Shaw ordered his soldiers to form two lines of battle, fix bayonets, and lie down on the sand. The men exchanged letters, shook hands with each other, reminded others whom to write in case they were killed or captured, and told friends which pocket held letters for whom. Shaw did not worry about being lost or misidentified if the worst happened. Still, he wrote two short letters sending love to his mother and sisters and comforting himself that "We hear nothing but praise of the Fifty-fourth on all hands." For safekeeping, he left the letters and some papers with the Boston abolitionist and newspaper correspondent Edward Pierce. Pierce promised to make sure Shaw's father got them if anything happened. Riding back to his regiment and dismounting, Shaw walked up and down among the men, smoked a cigar, and talked with them in a most friendly way. Corporal Gooding remembered that he had never seen Shaw so informal with the soldiers. Shaw sat with this group and that, reminded them that nothing like what they were about to do had been done before, and warned them that the world was watching. With lips compressed and with a slight twitch at the corner of his mouth, Shaw challenged the men to "take the fort or die there." They swore to try.[1]

The bombardment stopped at seven o'clock. Thirty minutes later, Strong made a short speech to the men and ordered Shaw to advance. With a final admonition to "prove yourselves men," Shaw positioned himself in front and ordered, "Forward." Years later, one soldier remembered that the regiment fought even harder because Shaw was in front, not behind. They marched ahead until the batteries of Wagner and Sumter opened up at about two hundred yards from the fort. Correctly, Shaw ordered "double quick" and the regiment surged across the beach. At eighty yards the seventeen hundred Confederate defenders, who had been barely hurt by the nine-thousand-shell bombardment, unleashed grape shot and cannister. Lieutenant Grace said later: "Our men fell like grass before a sickle." Lieutenant Wilkie James said that the "battle line melted away" and the place became "a fiery furnace . . . a phalanx of defeat and death." The men waded knee deep through seawater, crossed a deeper moat, tore through abatis, and climbed up the sloping sand walls of Wagner as rifle fire blazed against them.[2]

With a small group of men, Shaw somehow made it to the top of the parapet before an enemy bullet killed him and dropped his body into the fort. Those near him remembered his last words differently, but they agreed that Shaw had waved his sword and urged his men forward. Nearly half the regiment succeeded in pushing its way inside Wagner and desperately held their ground on the wall for almost an hour before being forced to withdraw. The white troops supporting them were also unable to remove the defenders from the strong position. The Confederates lost 174 men. Of the 600 men of the Fifty-fourth who charged the fort, 272 were killed, wounded, or captured. Additional casualties from the white regiments brought Union losses to 1,515. Confederate gravediggers buried 800 Union soldiers in the sand in front of the fort the morning after the battle. Showing the contempt Southern whites held for the "principle line of the Abolitionists"—white officers leading black soldiers—the fort's commander, General Johnson Hagood, ordered Shaw thrown into a ditch with his men. The diggers made a trench, dropped Shaw's body in it, threw the bodies of twenty of his men face down on top of him, and shoveled them over with sand. Morris Island lived up to its earlier name: old maps showed it as "Coffin Land."[3]

The survivors of the Fifty-fourth struggled through the sand away from Fort Wagner, found friends, and re-formed at the southern end of Morris Island, where the sand dunes played out onto the flat beach near the Atlantic Ocean. Luis Emilio, the only officer above the rank of captain not wounded or killed in the attack, commanded the regiment. Wilkie James, twice wounded, crawled along with William Appleton until they reached the sea and safety. Men hugged one another, thanked God for their lives, and wept over the dead. They worried what the Confederates might do to their captured comrades and prayed that Shaw had somehow survived his wounds and would be returned by prisoner exchange. Since the fight on James Island on the sixteenth, the men had been in motion. Now they rested, but only for one day.[4]

Many wrote hurried notes telling loved ones that no matter what the papers reported, they were alive. In a letter to his fiancée two days after the assault, Sergeant-Major Lewis Douglass "snatched a moment to write." He knew they had passed the test and cast off the burden of proving themselves capable of fighting like white men. Rightfully proud that the Fifty-fourth had "established its reputation as a fighting regiment," Douglass told her, "not a man flinched." He understood the futility of the assault even as he wanted more: "Men fell all around me. A shell would explode and clear a space of twenty feet, our men would close up again, but it was no use we had to retreat. . . . How I got out of that fight alive I cannot tell, but I am here. . . . Remember if I die I die in a good cause. I wish we had a hundred thousand colored troops we would put an end to this war."[5]

The men of the Fifty-fourth were proud of what they had done and determined to do more. Just after the fight, several remarked that they would continue until "the last brother breaks his chains." Some said, "If all our people get their freedom, we can afford to die." Private Francis Myers, a twenty-three-year-old laborer from Paterson, New Jersey, who was wounded in the attack, expressed best what many felt: "Oh, I thank God so much for the privilege." The men justified the expectations of their officers and convinced all but the most skeptical critics of their bravery. Instead of being objects to which things happened, these men had been actors who changed their times. And they wanted more. Two weeks after Wagner, Sergeant Albanus Fisher declared: "I still feel more Eager for the struggle than I ever yet have, for I now wish to have Revenge for our galant Curnel." Like others before them, once blood spilled around them, black soldiers grew more determined to continue to the finish. The men participated in the siege that brought the fall of Wagner on September 6, 1863, then continued to serve their country for the remainder of the war. They always remembered the "little colonel" who sacrificed his life for a promise of better lives for black people. In the hospital at Beaufort, one of Shaw's men told Charlotte Forten, "He was one of the very best men in the world." Another teacher and nurse, Laura Towne, confided to her journal that the wounded men were "all greatly excited about him, hoping, fearing, disregarding their own wounds in their anxiety for him." Towne concluded with simple elegance, "They love him."[6]

Inside and outside the hospital tents, Dr. Ripley Stone treated the injured, sending the more seriously wounded to the better-staffed medical facilities around Beaufort. There, Sea Island blacks, who had interacted with the Northern black soldiers since the arrival in June, could not be stopped from bringing in wagonloads of melons and potatoes and caring for the men who were, as one of the exslaves said so eloquently, "wounded for we." And there Charlotte Forten left her schoolhouse duties to help nurse the men. When news of the battle reached her, Forten put her thoughts in her journal: "It is too terrible, too terrible to write. We only hope it may not all be true. That our noble, beautiful young Colonel is killed and the reg[iment] cut to pieces! I cannot, cannot believe it. . . . But oh, I am stunned, sick at heart. I can scarcely write. . . . And oh, I still must hope that our colonel, *ours* especially he seems to me, is not killed." Forten bolstered the wounded men's morale and her own by repeating the rumor — or hope — that Shaw "was not dead, but had been taken prisoner by the rebels." With that news, Forten recorded, "How joyfully their wan faces lighted up!" A few days later, after receiving definite news of Shaw's fate, she confided to her journal that it "makes me sad, sad at heart. . . . I know it was a glorious death." Forten also grieved for Shaw's "young wife" and mother, while she herself thought of the time "a little more than a week ago [when] I parted with him, after an exciting horseback ride, how strong, how well, how vigorous he was then." Shaw had given orders to Hallowell that if he died at Wagner, one of his horses should be presented to Charlotte Forten, a gift she treasured "most sacredly, all my life long." [7]

Obviously, the assault was ill conceived and, if judged on a military basis or on the loss of lives, a failure. If judged by its scale as compared to other battles of the war, it would attract little notice. But the charge upon Wagner changed things. Blacks had proven themselves as fighting men and vindicated their sponsors, the abolitionists. By year's end sixty black regiments were being organized, and they would not be used simply to dig fortifications, handle baggage, and cook food for white soldiers. They would be allowed to fight.

31 Aftermath: Fifty-fourth Massachusetts Infantry

ON JULY 20 those who had not been wounded were at work again, cooperating with white regiments on guard duty and in digging the siege trenches that would zig and zag the Union line forward toward Fort Wagner and beyond, to Charleston. After three full days of scooping sand, the men closed the 1,350-yard separation to 400 yards. The day before Forten got the word, confirmation of Shaw's death and burial reached the regiment as well as word that no black prisoners would be exchanged. Colonel M. S. Littlefield of the Fourth South Carolina (Colored) Infantry assumed temporary command of the regiment. Toward the end of the month, Norwood Hallowell arrived with the Fifty-fifth Massachusetts, camped on Folly Island, and undoubtedly raised spirits with news from home, consolations, and praise. At the same time, Brigadier General Edward Wild's First North Carolina Colored Infantry increased spirits by bringing more black fighting men into position against the Charleston defenses.[1]

Still, the birthplace of the rebellion would not yield to Union pressure until February 1865, even though the siege against Wagner brought the fort's evacuation on September 7. By that time, fifty-eight days after the ground assault, the daily bombardment by Union monitors and land batteries had raised, in the words of a Confederate defender, "an intolerable stench from the unearthed dead." The Confederates climbed aboard boats and left Fort Wagner to Union troops.[2]

The men of the Fifty-fourth walked into this ground hallowed by their comrades' lives and by their efforts to gain respect as men of war. Perhaps expressing best what most believed, Lieutenant Wilkie James, twice wounded in the assault, wrote that Wagner "was the culmination of our hopes and our toils, the point above all other points to which we had been climbing from the moment the negro soldier at Readville took the musket in his hand." Though proud, the men worried over what the Confederates might do to those who had been captured. They took some solace in Lincoln's order to protect African American captives: "For every soldier of the United States killed in violation of the laws of war, a rebel soldier shall be executed, and for every one enslaved by the enemy or sold into slavery, a rebel soldier shall be placed at hard labor on the public works." There is no proof that Confederates killed or enslaved any Fifty-fourth prisoners except for those who died from wanting for provisions and attention at Andersonville and other prisons.[3]

The regiment occupied the fort until January 1864 and regained strength as men arrived from Boston to refill the ranks. Edward Hallowell, healed of his three wounds and promoted to colonel, took command of the men. For the next eighteen months the unit would fight in the Department of the South, most notably at the Battles of Olustee, James Island, and Honey Hill. In early 1865 the regiment pulled garrison duty in Savannah. Later, in Charleston, the men quartered in the Citadel. The Fifty-fourth celebrated Independence Day in the city that most symbolized resistance to their freedom with a reading of the Emancipation Proclamation as a corrective addition to the Declaration of Independence.

On August 20 the regiment was officially mustered out of service. Within twenty-four hours the men were in a transport bound for home. Six days later, Brevet Brigadier General Hallowell and half the regiment arrived at Gallop's Island in Boston Harbor. The rest of the men joined them on August 29. On September 2, after being ferried to Commercial Wharf, the Fifty-fourth formed into ranks and marched toward the State House and Boston Common. Completing the circle of service, this parade was most unlike the one in May 1863, when everything stood in the balance, when they had yet to grieve for Shaw and the others, when "boys" had not proven themselves men, when the war had not turned.[4]

Edward Hallowell was at the front of the regiment. He had been just a length behind Shaw on that recent yet so long ago May; but unlike Shaw, he led not enthusiastic, untried, and nervous men, but, in Emilio's words, men who marched "with the swing . . . and the bearing of seasoned soldiers." No dissenters booed or yelled racial epithets this time; no one dared do such a thing. These were the men who for eighteen months had refused to accept lesser pay than Congress gave to its white soldiers. Congress finally agreed that fighting men—black and white—deserved equal compensation. The Fifty-fourth had forced parity by its courage on the sloping sand of Wagner and by proven dedication to the Union in the face of appalling discrimination.[5]

Conspicuous in the regimental ranks marched Sergeant William H. Carney, whose deeds at Wagner would garner the Medal of Honor. First Lieutenant Stephen A. Swails, the first African American to be commissioned an officer in the army, was the pride of his company. Peter Vogelsang and Frank Welch, also lieutenants and also black, marched alongside their men. They strode into the Common and stopped to perform the manual of arms for themselves and for the crowd. After a short speech in which he thanked them and hoped for their future as citizens in every state, Hallowell led his men to a feast of celebration at the Charles Street Mall, where he disbanded them for the last time.[6]

32 Aftermath: Shaw's Family

SHAW'S FAMILY GRIEVED their loss but were consoled by the many letters that mourned with them or glorified their son. Charles Lowell interpreted Robert's death as "a perfect ending. I see now that the best Colonel of the best black regiment had to die, it was a sacrifice we owed,—and how could it have been paid more gloriously?" Lowell told Harry Sturgis Russell that Shaw had died "for a cause greater than any National one." Edward Pierce fullfilled his promise by forwarding Shaw's last letters. Pierce consoled Shaw's parents: "With the opening of the war, your son gave himself to his country, and he has now laid down his life for a race." Lydia Maria Child comforted Sarah Shaw with the thought that Shaw had "died nobly in the defence of great principles, and has gone to join the glorious army of martyrs." Sarah already believed that. Later, Francis Shaw became convinced too, and he wrote his old friend William Lloyd Garrison, "We do thank God that our darling . . . was chosen, among so many equals, to be the martyred hero of the downtrodden of our land."[1]

When Francis and Sarah heard the news that Shaw was "buried with his niggers," Francis immediately wrote to Pierce that they could hope for "no holier place" for Shaw's body. Three days later, Francis sent more explicit instructions to the regimental surgeon, Dr. Lincoln Stone: "We mourn over our own loss & that of the

Regt, but find nothing else to regret in Rob's life, death or burial. We would not have his body removed from where it lies surrounded by his brave & devoted soldiers, if we could accomplish it by a word. Please to bear this in mind & also, let it be known, so that, even in case there should be an opportunity, his remains may not be disturbed." Shaw also wrote to General Gillmore and told him: "You will forbid the desecration of my son's grave." Because of the father's plea, when Fort Wagner fell to Union arms one month later, the grave remained undisturbed. Undoubtedly, the parents' action led to even higher praise for Shaw and the regiment, as the burial symbolized and symbolizes still the brotherhood of man.

Much later, the poet William Moody celebrated the mass burial. He also understood how death and glory helped raise a race to manhood and equality:

> They swept, and died like freemen on the height,
> Like freemen, and like men of noble breed;
> And when the battle fell away at night
> By hasty and contemptuous hands were thrust
> Obscurely in a common grave with him
> The fair-haired keeper of their love and trust.
> Now limb doth mingle with dissolved limb
> In nature's busy old democracy.[2]

Shaw's family carried on with life even while grieving over their loss. The Haggertys protected Annie from the early newspaper accounts and telegrams of Shaw's death until they confirmed the report. Nine months later Annie became a vivid symbol of her sacrifice and Shaw's when she reviewed the departure of New York's first black regiment. Until her death in 1907, Annie lived primarily in Switzerland and France, never remarried, and kept up a sporadic correspondence with Josephine Shaw Lowell.[3]

In the months following her brother's death, Josephine must

have recalled her diary entries of 1862 when she had yet to be touched by personal tragedy: "Delight fills my soul when I think of the noble fellows advancing, retreating, charging and dying." Josephine wrote once that Shaw told her he "expected to be 'slaughtered before it was over.'" Another entry announced that "martyrs are not to be pitied." In October 1864 Josephine, who had been married just twelve months and was eight months pregnant, learned that her husband, Charles Russell Lowell, had been killed in a cavalry charge at Cedar Creek. Earlier in the month he had written her, worrying, "I don't want to be shot till I've had a chance to come home. I have no idea that I shall be hit, but . . . it frightens me." As strong and determined as her mother, Josephine devoted herself to public service, worked for the New York State Board of Charities and Women's Municipal League, and wrote over fifty pamphlets to bring such issues as pauperism, asylums, unemployment, and children's and workers' rights before the public.[4]

Shaw's other sisters, Anna, Susanna, and Ellen, filled their lives with marriage and children. Susanna named her first son, born one month after Shaw's death, Robert Shaw Minturn. Anna stayed close to home while her husband, George Curtis, continued to write for *Harper's Weekly* and threw himself into the political questions of the day. After the war Ellen married her brother's old tutor, Major General Francis C. Barlow, and worked for civil service reform, African American education, and prison reform. Barlow became attorney general of New York and achieved fame when Winslow Homer used him as the model for the Union officer in *Prisoners at the Front.*[5]

Sarah and Francis Shaw were consoled by their son's bravery in a cause they had long advanced. They understood the symbolism in ensuring that his grave be undisturbed, allowing him to remain forevermore in a foreign soil. His burial tied up the idea of martyrdom they so respected in John Brown and now in their son. But the reality of losing a child coiled deeply within the mother. Sarah wrote to a longtime abolitionist and friend to tell him of the "treasure God had called upon us to lay upon His Altar—a treasure indeed it was, our only son. . . . I fully recognize that the cause for which he died is sacred to God & Humanity . . . [yet now] the cup of life for me is poisoned. The same sun no longer shines for me." Perhaps Sarah regretted that she had ever pushed him to do his duty as she believed it to be. Still she must have been comforted by the praise that others heaped upon her son's act and she would allow no one to call into question his devotion to his men.[6]

Further to bind up the wounds of war and to erase any stain from their son's name, the Shaws sent one thousand dollars to rebuild the Episcopal Church in Darien, Georgia, which had been destroyed along with the rest of the town when Colonel James Montgomery tried to burn away the sins of the slaveholding South. Sarah wrote the church's pastor, Reverend Robert F. Clute, pled for her son's innocence in the sack of Darien, and lamented, "Were I able I would rebuild the whole pretty town in his memory."[7]

Sarah continued to be the active matriarch of an ever-larger family that included fourteen grandchildren. Francis served as president of the National Freedmen's Relief Association, an organization that raised money and sent teachers to educate exslaves. He joined with Levi Coffin and others successfully to lobby Congress for the establishment of a Freedmen's Bureau. Throughout their lives the Shaws remained philanthropists and spokespersons for progressive reform. And they never really got over the loss of their son and the hero status they had helped construct for him. On the night of her death in 1902, Sarah Shaw stared into the face of Robert in the picture she always kept beside her bed and addressed him directly: "Rob, Rob, where are you?" Puzzled and grieving—and receiving no response that we know of—she half-blamed and half-demanded of him, "Why don't you come and get me?" Perhaps she rejoined her beloved son in the afterlife; certainly she believed she would.[8]

33 Glory

THE PROPAGANDA EFFECT of Wagner was enormous. The *New York Tribune* reported that the battle would be to black Americans what Bunker Hill was to white Americans. The influential *Atlantic Monthly* declared, "Through the cannon smoke of that dark night the manhood of the colored race shines before many eyes that would not see." The *Boston Commonwealth* tied the charge to John Brown by printing that the bodies of the men were "mouldering in the ground" and quoted a white soldier at Wagner as saying, "We don't know any black men here, they're all soldiers." The *Richmond County Gazette*, Staten Island's paper, quoted another white soldier at Morris Island in support of black troops and against those who still wanted only whites to fight: "We know men from monkeys. . . . If you have any blue or green men that can work and fight, send them along." The Northern population that accepted putting blacks into uniforms as a test now acknowledged that black men could fight and kill like white men. In 1935 W. E. B. Du Bois wrote about the change that the black soldier wrought on white minds: "How extraordinary . . . in the minds of most people . . . only murder makes men. The slave pleaded; he was humble; he protected the women of the South, and the world ignored him. The slave killed white men; and behold, he was a man."[1]

In fact, all the circumstances surrounding Shaw, his family, the abolitionist movement, the raising of the regiment, his youth, his marriage just eighty days before his death, his acceptance of an unpopular command, the sacrifice of life for human freedom, the death upon a parapet of a fort protecting Charleston, the burial and sneer—"with his niggers"—the comparison with John Brown, and his parents' response to it all, made him larger than life.

Few acts have been more right for memorial than Shaw's death and burial at Wagner. Hundreds of supporters gave money to build a monument in his honor. In 1863 the men and friends of the regiment in South Carolina contributed nearly three thousand dollars to build a memorial on Morris Island. But instead of a monument, the money was used to help finance a more useable remembrance, the Shaw School for black children in Charleston. Still, the martyr has traditional memorials. A granite column stands as a tombstone would in the Moravian Cemetery plot on Staten Island. Shaw's likeness and name appear alongside others on the wall to the alumni dead in Memorial Hall at Harvard University. And then, of course, there is the masterpiece by Augustus Saint-Gaudens.[2]

Dedicated on May 31, 1897, thirty-four years after the grand march from Boston, the monument depicts Shaw again leading his men toward recognition and glory. In 1897 sixty-five officers and men, most in their old uniforms, listened to the band play "John Brown's Body," heard William James and Booker T. Washington talk about sacrifice, and saluted the memorial, their fallen comrades, and one another. Most had read Luis Emilio's three-year-old history, *A Brave Black Regiment*, to which they had contributed their memories and anecdotes. Of the 1,354 men who served in the Fifty-fourth, 100 died of battle wounds, 19 perished in prison camps, 94 succumbed to disease or accident, and 57 were considered missing in action, probably dead.[3]

The year 1897 was only a focal point for the praise aimed at Shaw. Just eleven days after the storming of Wagner, Charles Sumner recognized that Shaw's "death will be sacred in history and art." New England's poets, writers, and editors—many of them friends or relatives of the Shaws—also recognized what Sumner knew. They wrote verses to Northern idealism and the fallen hero. Shaw's death symbolized their own moral conscience and they were quick to explain that to others. By so doing, they helped make Shaw one of the Civil War's most celebrated legends. Since his death, at least forty poems have been written to eulogize him, and he has become more monument than man.[4] Ralph Waldo Emerson wrote:

> So nigh is grandeur to our dust,
> So near to God is man,
> When Duty whispers low, *Thou must,*
> The youth replies, *I can.*[5]

Six months after Wagner, James Russell Lowell penned "Memoriae Positum: R.G.S., 1863":

> Brave, good, and true,
> I see him stand before me now.
> . . . .
> Right in the van,
> On the rampart's slippery swell
> With heart that beat a charge, he fell
> Foeward, as fits a man.[6]

A century after Lowell wrote his elegy, another Lowell composed "For the Union Dead" in order to compare the moral degeneration of modern Boston with the unselfish sacrifice of Shaw:

> He is out of bounds now. He rejoices in man's lovely,
> peculiar power to choose life and die—
> when he leads his black soldiers to death,
> he cannot bend his back.[7]

And so there is the monument on Boston Common. Shaw rides in step with his men. An angel of the Lord glides over them. The bronze breathes and challenges viewers to remember the American creed. Shaw deserved the monument for his steadfastness to honor, even though he never had the clear-eyed crusader's vision, commitment to abolition, faith in moral uplift, or deep-thinking ability of some in the antislavery movement. What Shaw had was courage and loyalty. He was responsible enough to give black troops a fair trial. He did his duty to his men, his mother, and himself.

Fortunate in birth and in war, Shaw grew stronger and developed a richer personal character after he accepted an unwanted position at the head of a black regiment and struggled with his own preconceptions of black inferiority. The men of the Fifty-fourth lifted him to a higher plane and educated him even as their efforts caused others to reexamine their own prejudices.

Fort Wagner has since been reclaimed by the sea, and the grave of Shaw and his men lie undisturbed by the footfalls of tourists. In this sense they belong to the world and are washed by the same waters that link the Americas to Africa and Europe. The ocean is such a powerful metaphor for life and equality that no better resting place can be conceived. That they died for one another, and that Saint-Gaudens could build the magnificent monument to their triumph over inequality, is just and proper.

William James explained the meaning of their sacrifice—and of Shaw's commitment to duty—when he looked upon the monument in 1897: "There they march, warm-blooded champions of a better day for man. There on horseback among them, in his very habit as he lived, sits the blue-eyed child of fortune." On that same occasion, Booker T. Washington told the assembled crowd that the "full measure of the fruit of Fort Wagner and all that this monument stands for will not be realized until every man covered by a black skin" has the unrestricted opportunity to succeed. That we have yet to enjoy the fruit of the lessons they tried to teach us is disheartening, but their sacrifice was not in vain. For as we strive to learn, Shaw and his men continue to march forward from Boston Common.[8]

ABBREVIATIONS

AHS	Annie Kneeland Haggerty (after May 2, 1863, Annie Haggerty Shaw).
ASC	Anna Shaw Curtis.
BECF	Russell Duncan, ed., *Blue-Eyed Child of Fortune: The Civil War Letters of Colonel Robert Gould Shaw* (New York: Avon Press, 1994).
BPL	Boston Public Library.
CMSR	Compiled Military Service Records, National Archives.
ES	Josephine (Effie) Shaw.
FGS	Francis George Shaw.
HL	Houghton Library, Harvard University.
LTRS	*Letters: RGS* (Cambridge: Harvard University Press, 1876).
LYM	T. Lyman III Collection. Massachusetts Historical Society.
MHS	Massachusetts Historical Society.
NA	National Archives.
NBFPL	New Bedford Free Public Library.
NYHS	New York Historical Society.
NYPL	New York Public Library.
NYDT	*New York Daily Tribune.*
NYT	*New York Times.*
OR	*The War of the Rebellion: A Compilation of the Official Records of the Union and Confederate Armies.* 128 vols. Washington, D.C.: U.S. Government Printing Office, 1880–1901.
RGS	Robert Gould Shaw.

RGS:COLL   Robert Gould Shaw Collection. Houghton Library. Harvard University.

SBS   Sarah Blake Shaw.

SHAW   Shaw, Robert Gould. *Letters: RGS.* Cambridge, Mass.: Harvard University Press, 1864.

SIHS   Staten Island Historical Society.

SIIAS   Staten Island Institute of Arts and Sciences.

SS   Susanna (Susie) Shaw (after Oct. 31, 1862, Susanna Shaw Minturn).

WVU   West Virginia University.

NOTES

PREFACE

1. RGS to SBS, Oct. 5, 1862, SHAW, 202.

2. James quoted from Gary Scharnhorst, "From Soldier to Saint: Robert Gould Shaw and the Rhetoric of Racial Justice." *Civil War History* 34 (Dec. 1988): 308.

CHAPTER 1. BOSTON COMMON

1. Among his many works, the sculptor Augustus Saint-Gaudens created exquisite statues of Abraham Lincoln, William Tecumseh Sherman, and David Farragut. In molding Shaw and the men of the Fifty-fourth, Saint-Gaudens hired many models and crafted forty heads before deciding on the twenty-one that stand in clear relief in the monument. Richard Benson, *Lay This Laurel: An Album on the Saint-Gaudens Memorial on Boston Common Honoring Black and White Men Together Who Served the Union Cause with Robert Gould Shaw and Died with Him July 18, 1863* (New York: Eakins, 1973); for an excellent look at the Shaw monument as seen through the eyes of the artist, see Homer Saint-Gaudens, ed., *The Reminiscences of Augustus Saint-Gaudens* (New York: Century, 1913).

2. *Douglass' Monthly* (Aug. 1863), quoted in James M. McPherson, *Battle Cry of Freedom: The Civil War Era* (Oxford: Oxford University Press, 1988), 564, for Sims see 83; Whittier quote from John B. Pickard, ed., *The Letters of John Greenleaf Whittier* (Cambridge, Mass.: Harvard University Press, 1975), 3:362.

CHAPTER 2. BRAHMIN CHILDHOOD

1. Robert T. Teamoh, *Sketch of the Life and Death of Colonel Robert Gould Shaw* (Boston: Boston Globe, 1904).

2. Ibid.; Marion W. Smith, *Beacon Hill's Colonel Robert Gould Shaw* (New York: Carlton Press, 1986), 491–92; Roger Faxton Sturgis, *Edward Sturgis of Yarmouth, Mass., 1613–1695, and His Descendants* (Boston: Stanhope, 1914), 50–54; W. P. Garrison and F. J. Garrison, *William Lloyd Garrison, 1805–1879: The Story of His Life* (New York: Century, 1889), 3:79–80.

3. Robert Gould Shaw (1776–1853) and Nathaniel Russell Sturgis (1779–1856). Shaw was one of only eighteen men in Massachusetts worth over one million dollars in 1852. Sturgis, *Edward Sturgis*, 50–51; Cleveland Amory, *The Proper Bostonians* (New York: E. P. Dutton, 1947), 20, 49, 209; Abner Forbes and J. W. Greene, *The Rich Men of Massachusetts* (Boston: Fetridge, 1852), 61; Mary C. Crawford, *Famous Families of Massachusetts* (Boston: Little, Brown, 1930), 1:242, 2:163; Lawrence Leder, *The Bold Brahmins: New England's War Against Slavery: 1831–1863* (New York: E. P. Dutton, 1961), 110; Joan Waugh, "Unsentimental Reformer: The Life of Josephine Shaw Lowell" (Ph.D. dissertation, University of California–Los Angeles, 1992), 15.

4. Waugh, "Unsentimental Reformer," 22; Forbes and Greene, *Rich Men*, 194; Richard M. Bayles, ed., *History of Richmond County (Staten Island) New York from Its Discovery to the Present Time* (New York: L. E. Preston, 1887), 572–74.

5. Bayles, *History of Richmond County*, 572; newspaper clipping from *Boston Transcript*, May 29, 1897, in Fifty-fourth Massachusetts Infantry Regiment Papers, MHS; Shaw's friend quoted in *Richmond County Gazette*, Nov. 28 (2:1–2), 1882 [in references to newspapers, page and column numbers are indicated in parentheses]; Lindsay Swift, *Brook Farm: Its Members, Scholars, and Visitors* (New York: Macmillan, 1900), 257; Francis George Shaw, trans., *The Children of the Phalanstery: A Familiar Dialogue on Education*, by Felix Cantegrel (New York: W. H. Graham, 1848), 6, expressed the danger of capitalism to future generations: "All things are bound together in nature, and if your social order engenders evil and infinite suffering for men and for women of all ranks and all conditions . . . so it is with children"; Francis George Shaw, trans., *The Life of Charles Fourier*, by Charles Pellarin (New York: W. H. Graham, 1848).

6. Francis George Shaw, "A Piece of Land," in Henry George, *Social Problems* (New York: J. W. Lovell, 1883), 298–304.

7. Article from *Sewanee Review* 39 (Apr.–June 1931): 131–42, in Robert Gould Shaw Collection, HL; Swift, *Brook Farm*, 19–25; Thomas Woodson, Neal Smith, and Norman H. Pearson, *Nathaniel Hawthorne: The Letters, 1843–1853* (Columbus: Ohio State University Press, 1985), 201, 238, 251; FGS to George Ripley, Feb. 1845, Dana Collection, MHS; George William Curtis, *From the Easy Chair* (New York: Harper, 1892), 3:14–15; George W. Cooke, *Unitarianism in America: A History of Its Origin and Development* (Boston: American Unitarian Association, 1902), 353–57, 382, 399, 428; George M. Frederickson, *The Inner Civil War: Northern Intellectuals and the Crisis of the Union* (New York: Harper & Row, 1965), 13.

CHAPTER 3. ABOLITIONIST UPBRINGING

1. Teamoh, *Sketch of Shaw*, 11; Milton Meltzer and Patricia Holland, eds., *Lydia Maria Child: Selected Letters, 1817–1880* (Amherst: University of Massachusetts Press, 1982), 85, 324–27; Lydia Maria Child, *Correspondence Between Lydia Maria Child and Gov. Wise and Mrs. Mason of Virginia* (Boston: American Anti-Slavery Society, 1860), reprinted in *Anti-Slavery Tracts* (Westport, Conn.: Greenwood Press, 1970); for the best of Child's letters to the Shaws, see Lydia Maria Child to FGS, June 2, 1854, Oct. 27, 1856, and Dec. 22, 1859, Sarah Blake Sturgis Shaw Papers, HL.

2. FGS, Wendell Phillips, et al., to Hon. Rufus Choate, Feb. 1, 1842, William Lloyd Garrison Papers, BPL; Walter M. Merrill and Louis Ruchames, eds., *The Letters of William Lloyd Garrison* (Cambridge, Mass.: Harvard University Press, 1979), 4:334–35.

3. Gay quoted in Peter Burchard, *One Gallant Rush: Robert Gould Shaw and His Brave Black Regiment* (New York: St. Martin's Press, 1965), 6; William R. Stewart, *The Philanthropic Work of Josephine Shaw Lowell* (New York: Macmillan, 1911), 1–3, quote by a neighbor (Joseph Choate), 3.

4. Waugh, "Unsentimental Reformer," 16–17.

CHAPTER 4. JESUIT EDUCATION

1. Charles W. Leng and William T. Davis, *Staten Island and Its People: A History, 1609–1929* (New York: Lewis Historical Publishing Co., 1929), 1:253–54; Charles G. Hine and William T. Davis, *Legends, Stories, and Folklore of Old Staten Island* (New York: Staten Island Historical Society, 1925), 26, 31, 36–37, 63, 64.

2. Vernon B. Hampton, *Staten Island's Claim to Fame* (Staten Island: Richmond Borough, 1925), 165; RGS to SBS, Oct. 20, 1850 and Dec. 6, 1852, *LTRS,* 7; Franklin B. Hough, comp., *Census of the State of New York for 1855* (Albany: Van Benthysen, 1857), p.xxxiii; Teamoh, *Sketch of Shaw,* 11–12.

3. Burchard, *One Gallant Rush,* 8.

4. RGS to SBS, June 3, 1850, Sept. 7, 17, and 29, 1850, and Oct. 3, 1850, RGS to FGS, Nov. 30, 1850, *LTRS,* 3–6, 8, 10.

5. RGS to SBS, Sept. 17, 1850, and Sept. 10, 1855, *LTRS,* 73.

6. RGS to SBS, Sept. 7 and 29, 1850, and Dec. 12, 1850; RGS to FGS, 20 October, 1850, *LTRS,* 4, 5, 7, 8, 12.

7. Fuller quoted from Waugh, "Unsentimental Reformer," 42.

CHAPTER 5. NEUCHÂTEL

1. RGS to FGS, Oct. 13, 1851, and July 7, 1853, RGS to SBS, [Oct. 13], 1851, *LTRS,* 13–15, 39.

2. RGS to SBS, Nov. 13, 1851, Feb. 28, 1852, Mar. 13, 1853, Apr. 14, 1853, and June 2, 1853, *LTRS,* 16–17, 22, 32, 33, 35.

3. RGS to SBS, [n.d.], 1851, Jan. 3, 1852, Mar. 13, 1853, Apr. 14, 1853, and June 12, 1853, RGS to SBS and FGS, Apr. 24, 1853, RGS to FGS, July 13, 1853, *LTRS,* 15, 18, 34, 36, 40; SBS to RGS, Dec. 6, 1852, RGS: COLL; Shaw probably was not as touched by *The Key to Uncle Tom's Cabin* as Frederick Douglass, who asserted, "There has not been an exposure of slavery so terrible"; in Harriet Beecher Stowe, *The Key to Uncle Tom's Cabin* (Boston: Jewett, 1853; reprint, New York: Arno Press, 1968), ii.

4. RGS to SBS, [n.d.] 1851, and Jan. 3, 1852, RGS to SBS and FGS, Mar. 21, 1852, *LTRS,* 15–16, 19, 23–24.

5. RGS to SBS, [n.d.] 1851, and Feb. 6, 1853, *LTRS,* 16, 30.

CHAPTER 6. HANOVER

1. RGS to SBS, July 25, 1853, *LTRS,* 41, 46n; RGS to AHS, June 9, 1863, SHAW, 299.

2. RGS to SBS, July 19, 1854, *LTRS,* 46, 47.

3. RGS to SBS, Oct. 8, 1854, Nov. 5 and 23, 1854, and July 16, 1855, RGS:COLL.

4. RGS to SBS, Nov. 23 and 27, 1854, Sept. 30, 1855, Oct. 7, 1855, and Jan. 30, 1856, *LTRS,* 59, 77, 79.

5. RGS to SBS, Aug. 1, 1853, and Feb. 27, 1855, *LTRS,* 42–43, 63.

6. RGS to SBS, Oct. 28, 1855, and Dec. 26, 1855, RGS to FGS, Mar. 5, 1856, RGS:COLL.

7. RGS to SBS, July 1, 1855, Dec. 31, 1855, Jan. 30, 1856, and Feb. 26, 1856, *LTRS,* 66, 94, 98, 101.

8. RGS to SBS, Dec. 11, 1855, *LTRS,* 86.

CHAPTER 7. HARVARD

1. RGS to SBS, Apr. 9, 1856, RGS:COLL; RGS to SBS, Oct. 14, 1855, and Apr. 9, 1856, *LTRS,* 80, 108.

2. RGS to FGS, Nov. 7, 1855, RGS to SBS, Feb. 20, 1856, and Mar. 15, 1856, *LTRS,* 83, 101, 105; Elliotville became West New Brighton in 1866, with Francis Shaw as one of its four trustees. Leng and Davis, *Staten Island,* 271, and H. F. Walling, "Map of Staten Island, 1859," SIHS; U.S. Census, Eighth Census (1860), New York, Richmond County, Castleton, 152; Hine and Davis, *Legends,* 54, 65–66, 77, 79; Hampton, *Staten Island's Claim,* 23–24, 74; J. J. Clute, *Annals of Staten Island from Its Discovery to the Present Time* (New York: Charles Vogt, 1877), 294–95; the Shaws leased pew 57 in the Unitarian church for two hundred dollars a year. Curtis Collection, SIIAS.

3. RGS to SBS, Aug. 29, 1856, and Dec. 2, 1857, RGS:COLL; RGS to SBS, Sept. 30, 1856, Apr. [n.d.], 1857, and Dec. 2, 1857, *LTRS,* 113, 121, 138; Thomas W. Higginson, *Harvard Memorial Biographies* (Cambridge, Mass.: Sever & Francis, 1867), 2:172.

4. RGS to SBS, Sept. 5, 1856, Oct. 7, 1856, Mar. 29, 1857, Apr. 22, 29, and [n.d.], 1857, May 11, 1857, June 3 and 22, 1857, Oct. [n.d.], 1857, Sept. 9, 1858, and Nov. [n.d.], 1858, RGS:COLL; RGS to SBS, Feb. 20,

1856, *LTRS,* 101; Walter R. Spalding, *Music at Harvard: A Historical Record of Men and Events* (New York: Coward-McCann, 1935), 71–74.

5. RGS to SBS, Mar. 14 and 29, 1857, Apr. [n.d.], 1857, and May 23, 1858, RGS:COLL. Helper's book called for the South's poor whites to unite against the slaveholders, because slavery gave them an advantage that harmed nonslaveholders.

6. RGS to SBS, Nov. 18, 1856, and Mar. 19, 1858, RGS:COLL.

CHAPTER 8. NYC BUSINESSMAN

1. RGS to SBS, Sept. 20, 1857, Oct. 31, 1857, Sept. 9, 1858, and Dec. 1 and 9, 1858; RGS to FGS, Mar. 24, 1858, RGS:COLL.

2. RGS to Heinrich [Henry Vezin], July 24, 1859, and Sept. 16, 1859, RGS:COLL; RGS to SBS, Jan. 25, 1860, *LTRS,* 157.

3. RGS to SBS, Mar. 29, 1861, RGS:COLL; RGS to SBS, Nov. 18, 1860, *LTRS,* 158.

CHAPTER 9. NEW YORK'S DARLING SEVENTH

1. RGS to SBS, Mar. 29, 1861, RGS:COLL.

2. William Swinton, *History of the Seventh Regiment National Guard, State of New York During the War of the Rebellion* (New York: Dillingham, 1886), 24–36; Emmons Clark, *History of the Seventh Regiment of New York, 1806–1889* (New York: Published by the author, 1890), 1:473–74; Theodore Winthrop lived on Staten Island with his sister. Gay quoted in Hine and Davis, *Legends,* 83; Ernest A. McKay, *The Civil War and New York City* (Syracuse: Syracuse University Press, 1990), 67–68.

3. RGS to SBS, June 9 and Sept. 5, 1861, RGS:COLL; RGS to SBS, June 16, 1861, SHAW.

4. RGS to SBS, Apr. 18 and 20, 1861, RGS:COLL; RGS to SS, Apr. 18, 1861, SHAW, 20; Clark, *History of the Seventh,* 1:473–74.

5. RGS to SBS, Apr. 18 and 23, 1861, RGS:COLL.

6. RGS to SBS, May 2, 1861, RGS:COLL.

7. RGS to SBS, Apr. 27, 1861, SHAW, 18.

8. Ibid.; RGS to SBS, May 2, 1861, RGS:COLL.

9. RGS to FGS, May 4, 1861, RGS:COLL.

CHAPTER 10. OFFICER RANK AND LOYALTY

1. RGS to SBS, May 19, 1861, SHAW, 35.

2. RGS to ASC, Sept. 23, 1861, and RGS to ES, July 31, 1861, Dec. 8, 1861, Jan. 15, 1862, and Feb. 9, 1862, RGS:COLL; RGS to FGS, Oct. 13, 1861, SHAW, 90.

3. RGS to FGS, May 13, 1862, and RGS to SBS, June 9, 1861, RGS:COLL; RGS to FGS, May 12, 1861, and RGS to ES, Nov. 21, 1862, RGS to AHS, Nov. 23 and 28, 1862, and RGS to SBS, Nov. 17, 1862, and Dec. 1, 1862, SHAW, 34, 44, 151–52, 212–13, 217, 222.

CHAPTER 11. JOHN BROWN AND A DISCIPLINED ARMY

1. For the best look at the heroization of Brown, which includes all the quotes, see Stephen B. Oates, *To Purge This Land with Blood: A Biography of John Brown* (Amherst: University of Massachusetts Press, 1984), 319–61.

2. RGS to SBS, March 3, 1862, SHAW, 126–27.

3. RGS to SBS, July 18, 1861, RGS:COLL; RGS to SBS, July 30, 1861, and RGS to Sydney Gay, August 6, 1861, SHAW, 58, 64.

4. RGS to SBS, Sept. 5, 1861, RGS:COLL.

5. RGS to FGS, Aug. 13, 1861, SHAW, 68; RGS to SBS, Aug. 30, 1861, and RGS to ES, Apr. 16, 1862, RGS:COLL.

6. RGS to SBS, Aug. 30, 1861, and RGS to ES, Sept. 11, 1861, RGS:COLL.

7. RGS to SBS, May 25, 1861, and Aug. 30, 1861, RGS:COLL; RGS to SBS, Mar. 14, 1862, and Sept. 25, 1862, SHAW, 130, 196.

8. RGS to ES, Jan. 15, 1862, RGS to SBS, Feb. 16, Apr. 11 and 19, and Sept. 25, 1862, SHAW, 115, 123, 140, 144, 196.

CHAPTER 12. CAMP LIFE IN VIRGINIA

1. RGS to ES, July 31, 1861, Dec. 8, 1861, and Jan. 15, 1862, RGS to SBS, July 18 and 21, 1861, RGS:COLL; RGS to SBS, Apr. 19, 1862, SHAW, 143–44.

2. RGS to SBS, Sept. 5, 1861, and RGS to George W. Curtis, Oct. 8, 1861, RGS:COLL; RGS to Nellie (Ellen Shaw), Apr. 5, 1862, SHAW, 138.

3. RGS to ES, Dec. 8, 1861, and Jan. 15, 1862, RGS:COLL.

4. RGS to SS, Aug. 15, 1861, and RGS to ASC, Sept. 23, 1861, RGS: COLL; RGS to SBS, Dec. 25, 1861, SHAW, 112.

CHAPTER 13. WHAT WAR REALLY IS: ANTIETAM

1. RGS to SBS, Apr. 19, 1861, and July 28, 1862, SHAW, 143, 177.

2. RGS to SBS, Mar. 28, 1862, RGS:COLL.

3. RGS to FGS, May 27, 1862, RGS:COLL.

4. RGS to SBS, June 13, 1862, and July 23, 1862, SHAW, 160, 174–75; RGS to FGS, May 27, 1862, RGS:COLL; James M. McPherson, *For Cause and Comrades: Why Men Fought in the Civil War* (New York: Oxford University Press, 1997), 31.

5. RGS to SBS, June 19, 1862, SHAW, 162.

6. RGS to SBS, July 23, 1862, SHAW, 174–75.

7. RGS to FGS, Aug. 11, 1862, SHAW, 181.

8. *OR*, 1:12, pt. 2, 807–8; Bowen, *Massachusetts in the War*, 120; Krick, *Stonewall Jackson at Cedar Mountain*, 372–76; RGS to FGS, Aug. 11, 1862, and RGS to SBS, Aug. 12, 1862, SHAW, 181–85.

9. RGS to FGS, Sept. 21, 1862, SHAW, 191–93.

10. Ibid.

11. RGS to SBS, June 9, 1861, RGS:COLL; RGS to FGS, Sept. 21, 1862, SHAW, 193.

12. RGS to SBS, Mar. 28, 1862, and RGS to Annie [Russell Agassiz], Aug. 13, 1862, RGS:COLL; RGS to SBS, May 9, 1862, and Aug. 12, 1862, SHAW, 150, 184.

CHAPTER 14. ANNIE HAGGERTY

1. RGS to AHS, Nov. 28, 1862, SHAW, 221.

2. RGS to FGS, Nov. 23, 1861, SHAW, 105; *BECF*, 163n.

3. RGS to AHS, Nov. 28, 1862, and RGS to ES, Dec. 23, 1862, SHAW, 220, 233.

4. RGS to AHS, Dec. 21, 1862, SHAW, 230.

5. RGS to AHS, Feb. 18, 1863, SHAW, 262.

6. RGS to SS, Aug. 15 and Sept. 17, 1861, SHAW, 71, 84; RGS to Mimi [Elizabeth Russell Lyman], Feb. 20, 1863, LYM; obituary of Ogden Haggerty, *NYT*, Sept. 1 (4:7), 1875.

7. RGS to SS, Aug. 15, 1861, SHAW, 71.

8. RGS to AHS, Nov. 23, 1862, and RGS to SBS, Nov. 21, 1862, and Dec. 1, 1862, SHAW, 216, 217; ASC to Mimi, Feb. 16, 1863, Lyman Family Papers, 1785−1956, Reel 13, No. 14.2, MHS.

9. RGS to SBS, Dec. 1, 1862, and Dec. 23, 1862, and RGS to AHS, Dec. 18, 1862, and Feb. 4, 1863, SHAW, 223, 228, 256.

10. RGS to AHS, Nov. 28, 1862, Jan. 25, 1863, and Feb. 4, 1863, RGS to ES, Dec 23, 1862, RGS to SBS, Jan. 23, 1863, SHAW, 220−21, 233, 250, 252, 253, 256; RGS to ES, Jan. 25, 1863, RGS:COLL; *BECF,* 278n.

CHAPTER 15. EMANCIPATION PROCLAMATION

1. RGS to SBS, July 18 and 21, 1861, RGS:COLL; RGS to SBS, Sept. 25, 1862, and Oct. 5, 1862, RGS to Mr. [Sydney] Gay, Aug. 6, 1861, RGS to FGS, Aug. 3 and Nov. 13, 1862, RGS to ES, Jan. 15 and Nov. 21, 1862, SHAW, 66, 142, 179, 196, 202, 211, 214.

2. *Douglass' Monthly* (May 1861), quoted in Dudley T. Cornish, "To Be Recognized as Men: The Practical Utility of History," *Military Review* 58 (Feb. 1978): 46; FGS to William Lloyd Garrison, May 16, 1862, William Lloyd Garrison Papers, BPL.

3. "U.S. Electors to Abraham Lincoln," Dec. 24, 1862, in *Letters and Recollections of John Murray Forbes,* ed. Sarah Forbes Hughes (Boston: Houghton Mifflin, 1899), 1:344−46.

4. Charles B. Sedgwick to J. M. Forbes, Dec. 22, 1862, in Hughes, *John Murray Forbes,* 1:347−48.

5. William F. Fox, *Regimental Losses in the American Civil War, 1861−1865* (Albany, N.Y.: Albany Publishing Co., 1889), 53; Ira Berlin, Joseph P. Reidy, and Leslie S. Rowland, eds., *Freedom: A Documentary History of Emancipation, 1861−1867,* series II: *The Black Military Experience* (Cambridge: Cambridge University Press, 1982), 12; Martin Binkin and Mark J. Eitelberg, *Blacks and the Military* (Washington, D.C.: Brookings Institution, 1982), 14−15.

CHAPTER 16. SOLDIERS OF AFRICAN DESCENT

1. Richard H. Abbott, "Massachusetts and the Recruitment of Southern Negroes, 1863−1865, *Civil War History* 14 (Sept. 1968): 197−98; J. M. Forbes to Governor Andrew, Jan. 22, 1863, John Albion Andrew

Papers, MHS; *NYT,* Jan. 9, 1863, quoted in Cornish, *The Sable Arm,* 96–97; *Annual Report of the Adjutant-General of the Commonwealth of Massachusetts . . . for the Year Ending Dec. 31, 1863* (Boston: Wright & Potter, 1864), 54–55.

2. William Schouler, *A History of Massachusetts in the Civil War* (Boston: E. P. Dutton, 1868), 1:407–8; *NYT,* June 6 (4:2), 1863; Phineas C. Headley, *Massachusetts in the Rebellion* (Boston: Walker, Fuller, 1866), 449; Douglass's speech quoted in John W. Blassingame, ed., *The Frederick Douglass Papers* (New Haven, Conn.: Yale University Press, 1985), 3:566–67.

CHAPTER 17. GOD'S WORK

1. Hughes, *John Murray Forbes,* 2:67; J. M. Forbes to Governor Andrew, Jan. 30, 1863, newspaper clipping of obituary of Morris Hallowell, June 17, 1880, Norwood P. Hallowell Papers and Scrapbooks, 1764–1914, MHS, *BECF,* 291n.

2. John A. Andrew to FGS, Jan. 30, 1863, J. A. Andrew Papers, MHS. Also printed in full in Luis F. Emilio, *A Brave Black Regiment: History of the Fifty-fourth Regiment of Massachusetts Volunteer Infantry, 1863–1865* (Boston: Boston Book Co., 1891; reprint, New York: Arno Press, 1969), 3–5.

3. John A. Andrew to FGS, Jan. 30, 1863, J. A. Andrew Papers, MHS.

4. Ibid., John A. Andrew to Capt. Robert Gould Shaw, Jan. 30, 1863; Higginson, *Harvard Memorial Biographies,* 2:189.

5. Charles Morse to [?], Feb. 8, 1863, Charles F. Morse, *Letters Written During the Civil War, 1861–1865* (Boston: Privately printed, 1898), 119–21. In July 1863 Morse had the opportunity to take a colonelcy in a black regiment, but he refused. See his letters, 142–43; RGS to AHS, Feb. 4, 1863, SHAW, 256.

6. RGS to SBS, Aug. 8, 1861, and RGS to FGS, May 19, 1862, SHAW, 65, 152–53; after Copeland's dismissal, Andrew tried to intervene on his behalf and probably first thought of him for the colonelcy. About the same time Shaw accepted the position, Andrew wrote Senator Sumner, asking, "What is Decided about Copeland?" See Andrew to Sumner, Feb. 9, 1863, in Berlin, *Black Military Experience,* 337; RGS file, CMSR, George L. Andrews Papers, United States Military History Institute.

7. Richard Cary to Helen [Cary], Oct. 16, 1861, and Jan. 16, 1862, Richard Cary Papers, MHS; Henry Lee Higginson, *The Soldier's Book* (Boston: Privately printed, 1890), n.p. [Savage section]; Higginson, *Harvard Memorial Biographies*, 1:305–26, Shaw's comment on Savage, 326.

8. Higginson, *Harvard Memorial Biographies*, 2:189; RGS to SBS, Oct. 14, 1862, and RGS to AHS, Feb. 4, 1863, SHAW, 206, 216, 256; SBS to RGS, Jan. 31, 1863, quoted in Robert Shaw Sturgis Whitman, "The 'Glory' Letters," *Berkshire (Mass.) Eagle*, Feb. 2 (6:2), 1990. Whitman's grandfather Robert Sturgis was a first cousin of Robert Gould Shaw.

9. RGS to AHS, Nov. 23, 1862, and Feb. 4, 1863, SHAW, 216, 256.

10. RGS to FGS, Feb. 6, 1863, in Teamoh, *Sketch of Shaw*, 16.

11. Oration by William James in *The Monument to Robert Gould Shaw: Its Inception, Completion, and Unveiling, 1865–1897* (Boston: Houghton Mifflin, 1897), 77–85.

12. SBS's letter to Governor Andrew quoted in Burchard, *One Gallant Rush*, 73; SBS to RGS, Feb. 6, 1863, RGS:COLL; Governor Andrew to FGS, Feb. 6, 1863, two telegrams in Hallowell Papers, MHS; John A. Andrew to RGS, Feb. 7, 1863, and John A. Andrew to E. M. Stanton, Feb. 9, 1863, Andrew Papers, MHS.

13. Higginson, *Four Addresses*, 90; *Memorial: RGS*, 6; John A. Andrew to James B. Congdon, Feb. 9, 1863, Soldier's Fund Committee, Scrapbook, James Bunker Congdon, NBFPL; ASC to Mimi [Elizabeth Russell Lyman], Feb. 16, 1863, Lyman Family Papers, MHS; *BECF*, 287n.

CHAPTER 18. MEN OF COLOR, TO ARMS!

1. ASC to Mimi [Elizabeth Russell Lyman], Feb. 1, 1863, Lyman Family Papers, MHS; Charles Lowell to Mother, Feb. 4 and 9, 1863, Charles Lowell to H. L. Higginson, Feb. 15, 1863, in Edward W. Emerson, *Life and Letters of Charles Russell Lowell* (Boston: Houghton Mifflin, 1907), 233, 235–36.

2. Wells and Garnett quoted from Donald Yacovone, ed., *Voice of Thunder: The Civil War Letters of George E. Stephens* (Urbana: University of Illinois Press, 1997), 30; newspaper clipping, *Boston Herald*, Feb. 17, 1863, in Hallowell Papers, MHS.

3. Charles E. Heller, "George Luther Stearns," *Civil War Times Illustrated* 13 (July 1974): 20–28; William S. McFeely, *Frederick Douglass*

(New York: W. W. Norton, 1990), 223; *Boston Commonwealth*, Feb. 22 (3:3), 1863; newspaper clipping of *Boston Transcript*, Feb. 17, 1863, in Hallowell Papers, MHS.

4. Advertisements from newspaper clippings in Hallowell Papers and Scrapbooks, MHS; *Boston Daily Journal*, Feb. 14 (2:4), 1863; Subscription Paper, Feb. 13, 1863, Scrapbook, Soldier's Fund Committee, NBFPL. The committee expanded and eventually had about one hundred members.

5. At least one newspaper reporter put Forbes in charge of the committee: "It is curious to see a meeting of the Committee on the Enlistment of Colored Troops. John M. Forbes is its chairman, a man of headlong energy, longtime an abolitionist, and more than any other man the confidential adviser and helper of Governor Andrew." Hughes, *John Murray Forbes*, 1:10; *Boston Commonwealth*, Apr. 10 (2:2–3), 1863; RGS to James B. Congdon, Mar. 17, 1863, Scrapbook, Soldier's Fund Committee, NBFPL; Henry Greenleaf Pearson, *The Life of John A. Andrew, Governor of Massachusetts, 1861–1865* (Boston: Houghton Mifflin, 1904), 2: 82; Berlin, *Black Military Experience*, 93, 98, 101–2; *BECF*, 291n.

6. *National Anti-Slavery Standard*, Feb. 14 (1:5, 3:1), 1863; McFeely, *Frederick Douglass*, 48; David W. Blight, *Frederick Douglass' Civil War: Keeping Faith in Jubilee* (Baton Rouge: Louisiana State University Press, 1989), 158; *BECF*, 291n.

CHAPTER 19. THE OFFICERS

1. Telegram, J. A. Andrew to N. P. Hallowell, Hallowell Papers, MHS; Teamoh, *Sketch of Shaw*, 17–18; J. M. Forbes to J. A. Andrew, Feb. 2, 1863, Andrew Papers, MHS; RGS to FGS, Mar. 21, 1863, RGS:COLL; RGS to AHS, Feb. 8, 1863, SHAW, 258.

2. RGS to Mimi (Russell), Feb. 20, 1863, LYM; RGS to Charley (Lowell), Feb. 21, 1863, MHS; J. W. M. Appleton to Col. T. W. Higginson, Jan. [n.d.], 1863, George L. Stearns to Col. T. W. Higginson, Jan. 20, 1863, Memoir of J. W. M. Appleton, Letterbook, J. W. M. Appleton Papers, 1861–1913, WVU.

3. Simpkins quoted in Burchard, *One Gallant Rush*, 78; William H. Simpkins file, CMSR.

4. Garth W. James, "The Assault upon Fort Wagner," in *War Papers read before the Commandery of the State of Wisconsin, Military Order of*

the Loyal Legion of the U.S. (Milwaukee: Burdick, Armitage & Allen, 1891), 9−10; Cabot [Russel] to Father, Mar. 8, 1863, Cabot Jackson Russell Papers, 1859−1865, NYPL; *BECF,* 333n.

5. RGS to John A. Andrew, Apr. 8, 1863, RGS:COLL; RGS to Col. [Francis L.] Lee, Apr. 9, 1863, in William A. Gladstone, *United States Colored Troops, 1863−1867* (Gettysburg, Pa.: Thomas Publications, 1990), 35; Appleton Scrapbook, 3−4, WVU; William Nutt, a first sergeant in the Second, was the only man to be commissioned in the Fifty-fourth from that regiment. Emilio, *A Brave Black Regiment,* 337; RGS to FGS, Mar. 21, 1863, RGS:COLL.

CHAPTER 20. THE RECRUITS

1. Emilio, *A Brave Black Regiment,* 19, 373; John M. Langston, *From Virginia Plantation to the National Capital* (Hartford, Conn.: American Publishing Co., 1894; reprint, New York: Johnson Reprint Corp., 1968), 200, 203; newspaper clipping from *Oberlin News,* Hallowell Papers, MHS; *National Anti-Slavery Standard,* Apr. 25 (3:2), 1863, May 2 (3:2), 1863.

2. *New Bedford Daily Mercury,* Feb. 18 (2:2), Feb. 20 (2:2), 1863; William H. Carney to Col. M. S. Littlefield, Oct. 16, 1863, newspaper clipping, Hallowell Papers, MHS; James H. Gooding file, CMSR; Emilio, *A Brave Black Regiment,* 349, 350. Virginia Adams has compiled the letters of James Gooding into *On the Altar of Freedom: A Black Soldier's Civil War Letters from the Front* (Amherst: University of Massachusetts Press, 1991).

3. *New Bedford Mercury,* Mar. 9 (2:2), and Mar. 11 (2:2), 1863.

4. Two newspaper clippings in Hallowell Papers, one dated Apr. 4, 1863, the other undated, MHS; Stephens quoted from Yacovone, *Voice of Thunder,* 33−34; James M. McPherson, *The Struggle For Equality: Abolitionists and the Negro in the Civil War and Reconstruction* (Princeton, N.J.: Princeton University Press, 1964), 206.

5. RGS to FGS, Apr. 2 and 24, 1863, RGS:COLL; *BECF,* 320n.

CHAPTER 21. CAMP MEIGS

1. *BECF,* 300n.

2. James, "Assault upon Fort Wagner," 13; *New Bedford Mercury,* Mar. 24 (2:3), 1863; *Annual Report of the Adjutant-General of Massachu-*

setts, 13; Adams, *On the Altar of Freedom*, 8; First Lieutenant Cabot Russel wrote his father that the men "have begun to die all ready" because of lung inflammation from close quarters and indoor drill. Cabot [Russel] to Father, Mar. 23, 1863, Russell Papers, NYPL; RGS to FGS, Apr. 2, 1863, RGS:COLL.

3. Norwood P. Hallowell, *The Negro as a Soldier in the War of the Rebellion* (Boston: Little, Brown, 1897), 9; newspaper clipping, "54th Mass. at Readville," in Hallowell Papers, MHS; Emilio, *Brave Black Regiment*, 22–23; RGS to Charley [Morse], Feb. 24, 1863, MHS; RGS to SBS, Mar. 17, 1863, SHAW, 273.

4. Newspaper clipping, "54th Mass. at Readville," in Hallowell Papers, MHS; General Order No. 1, HQ 54th Mass., Camp Meigs, Readville, Mar. 5, 1863, by command of Robert G. Shaw, Capt Cmdg 54th, and General Order No. 5, Records of the Adjutant General's Office, Record Group 94, Bound Record Books, 54th Massachusetts Infantry (Colored), Order Book, NA; General Order No. 12, Special Order Book, Camp Meigs Papers, NBFPL; *New Bedford Mercury*, Mar. 24 (3:2), 1863; Appleton Scrapbook, 6, WVU.

5. *New Bedford Mercury*, Mar. 8 (2:3), 1863; requisition for the Fifty-fourth Massachusetts, Feb. 19, 24, and 27, 1863, Mar. 4 and 5, 1863, Apr. 6, 21, and 22, 1863, and May 6, 11, and 22, 1863, Camp Meigs Papers, NBFPL.

6. RGS to AHS, Feb. 8, 1863, SHAW, 258; RGS to FGS, Aug. 29, 1862, RGS:COLL.

7. Hallowell, *Negro as a Soldier*, 9; RGS to SBS, Mar. 25, 1863, RGS: COLL.

8. Appleton Scrapbook, 3, WVU; *New Bedford Mercury*, Apr. 6 (2:3), 1863; General Order No. 9, Brig-Gen R. A. Peirce, Mar. 26, 1863, Bound Record Books, 54th Mass., Record Group 94, NA; Dale's report quoted in Smith, *Beacon Hill's*, 403; newspaper clipping, "54th Mass. at Readville," in Hallowell Papers, MHS; McPherson, *For Cause and Comrades*, 46.

9. *National Anti-Slavery Standard*, Apr. 4 (3:1), Apr. 11 (3:4), Apr. 28 (3:4–5), 1863; *New Bedford Mercury*, Mar. 24 (2:3), Mar. 30 (2:3), Mar. 31 (2:3), 1863, Apr. 6 (2:3), Apr. 13 (2:3), Apr. 21 (2:3), 1863; Edwin S. Redkey, "Black Chaplains in the Union Army," *Civil War History* 33 (Dec. 1987): 332.

10. Lewis Jackson wrote his wife that the men were having trouble getting along in the Readville barracks. McFeely, *Frederick Douglass*, 224. Joseph T. Glatthaar, *Forged in Battle: The Civil War Alliance of Black Soldiers and White Officers* (New York: Free Press, 1990), 61. Grimes was a pastor of the African Methodist Episcopal Church and Jackson the preacher at the Salem Baptist Church. Adams, *On the Altar of Freedom*, 6, 8.

11. RGS to FGS, Apr. 24, 1863, RGS:COLL.

12. Appleton Scrapbook, 4–5, WVU; *New Bedford Mercury*, Mar. 24 (2:3), 1863.

13. William Schouler to John A. Andrew, June 19, 1863, and N. P. Hallowell to John Andrew, June 20, 1863, in Requisitions Book, Camp Meigs Papers, NBFPL; *Record of the Service of the Fifty-Fifth Regiment of Massachusetts Volunteer Infantry* (Cambridge, Mass.: John Wilson & Son, 1868), 2:101; William Jackson to Brig Gen R A Peirce, June 19, 1863, Special Order Book, Camp Meigs Papers, NBFPL; *New Bedford Mercury*, May 26 (2:2), 1863.

CHAPTER 22. A RACIAL EDUCATION

1. RGS to Charley Morse, Feb. 21 and Mar. 4, 1863, R. G. Shaw II Collection, MHS; RGS to Mimi [Elizabeth Russell Lyman], Feb. 20, 1863, T. Lyman III Collection, MHS; *BECF*, 305n.

2. RGS to AHS, Mar. 14, 1863, SHAW, 272; RGS to SBS, Mar. 25, 1863, RGS:COLL; RGS to A. A. Lawrence, Mar. 25, 1863, A. A. Lawrence Collection, MHS; newspaper clipping, Aug. 16, 1863, in Hallowell Papers, MHS; Forbes quoted from Yacovone, *Voice of Thunder*, 28.

3. Lydia Maria Child to Willie Haskins, Apr. 30, 1863, in Meltzer and Holland, *Lydia Maria Child*, 427; William Wells Brown, *The Negro in the American Rebellion: His Heroism and His Fidelty* (New York: Lee & Shepard, 1867), 203–4; *National Anti-Slavery Standard*, Aug. 8 (2:4), 1863; *New Bedford Mercury*, Aug. 29 (2:2), 1863; William S. McFeely, Foreword to *BECF*, xi; for the best discussion of the change black soldiers wrought upon white officers, see Glatthaar, *Forged in Battle*, esp. x–12, 79–108.

4. Newspaper clipping, *New Bedford Standard*, Apr. 8, 1863, in Scrapbook, Soldiers' Fund Committee, NBFPL; *New Bedford Mercury*, Apr. 6

(2:3), 1863; RGS to Governor [John A.] Andrew, Apr. 6, 1863, Miscellaneous Bound, MHS; RGS to SBS, Apr. 7 and 8, 1863, RGS:COLL.

5. Hallowell, *Negro as a Soldier*, 10; RGS to John (M. Forbes), June 3, 1863, RGS:COLL; *New Bedford Mercury*, Apr. 27 (2:3), 1863, May 6 (2:3), May 26 (2:2), 1863; Garrison, *William Lloyd Garrison*, 4:79.

6. *New Bedford Mercury*, May 6 (2:3), May 11 (2:4), 1863; newspaper clipping from *Springfield Republican* in *Memorial: RGS*, 18; Charles Lowell to ES, May 27, 1863, in Emerson, *Life and Letters of C. R. Lowell*, 248.

CHAPTER 23. ANNIE HAGGERTY SHAW

1. RGS to AHS, Mar. 3, 1863, RGS to SBS, Feb. 20, 1863, Mar. 17 and 27, 1863, and Apr. 1, 1863, RGS to FGS, Apr. 3, 1863, SHAW, 263, 269, 273, 276, 278, 279; SBS to RGS, Feb. 6, 1863, Sarah Blake Shaw Papers, HL.

2. RGS to SBS, Apr. 1, 1863, SHAW, 278; J. Glenn Gray, *The Warriors: Reflections on Men in Battle* (New York: Harper & Row, 1970), 62.

3. RGS to SBS, Mar. 25, 1863, and RGS to FGS, Apr. 24, 1863, RGS: COLL; RGS to SBS, Mar. 27, 1863, and RGS to FGS, Mar. 30, 1863, SHAW, 256, 277.

4. RGS to SBS, Apr. 14, 1863, RGS to ES, Mar. 3, 1863, RGS:COLL; RGS to Charley [Morse], Mar. 4, 1863, MHS.

5. RGS to Charley [Morse], May 3, 1863, MHS; RGS to ES, May 6, 1863, SHAW, 286.

6. RGS to SBS, Apr. 8 and 14, 1863, RGS to SS, May 7, 1863, *SHAW*, 282, 283, 287; RGS to Charley [Morse], May 3, 1863, MHS; *Trow's New York City Directory for the Year 1863*, 14; RGS to Mrs. Robert Gould Shaw, May 9, 1863, RGS to Ogden Haggerty, May 8, 1863, Robert Gould Shaw, Military and Personal Telegrams, NYHS.

CHAPTER 24. SO FINE A SET OF MEN

1. RGS to FGS, Mar. 30, 1863, SHAW, 277.

2. James Oliver Horton and Lois E. Horton, *Black Bostonians: Family Life and Community Struggle in the Antebellum North* (New York: Holmes & Meier, 1979), 127; *National Anti-Slavery Standard*, May 23

(3:5), 1863; *Boston Commonwealth,* May 22 (2:2–4), 1863; RGS to SBS, May 18, 1863, SHAW, 289.

3. Emilio, *Brave Black Regiment,* 25–30; RGS to SBS, May 18, 1863, SHAW, 289.

4. *National Anti-Slavery Standard,* June 6 (3:3), 1863; "Souvenir of the Massachusetts Fifty-fourth (Colored) Regiment" (Boston: 1863), 1; reporter quoted from *Commonwealth,* June 5 (2:1), 1863.

5. Jacobs quoted by Lydia Maria Child in *Memorial: RGS,* 168; SBS quoted from Shelby Foote, *The Civil War: A Narrative* (New York: Random House, 1963), 2:697; SBS to J. E. Cairnes, June 4, 1863, in Weinberg, *John Elliot Cairnes,* 164; SBS to RGS, May 31, 1863, RGS:COLL; A. A. Lawrence to Sarah A. Lawrence, May 28, 1863, Amos Adams Lawrence Papers, HL; Robert Rantoul, "A Reminiscence of War Times," in Garrison, *William Lloyd Garrison,* 4:80; Pickard, *Letters of Whittier,* 3:362.

6. Hallowell, *Negro as a Soldier,* 7; "Souvenir," 7; James, "Assault upon Fort Wagner," 13–14; RGS to John (M. Forbes), June 3, 1863, RGS: COLL.

7. *New Bedford Mercury,* May 29 (2:3), 1863; John Appleton to Mary [Appleton], May 28, 1863, two letters, Appleton Papers, WVU.

8. John Appleton to Mary [Appleton], May 28, 1863, two letters, Appleton Papers, WVU; Maj-Gen David Hunter to Gov [John A.] Andrew, May 4, 1863, and J. A. Andrew to E. M. Stanton, Apr. 1, 1863, in "The Negro in the Military Service of the United States, 1607–1889," Records of the Adjutant General's Office, Record Group 94, NA; *NYT,* May 17 (3:3), 1863.

9. John [Appleton] to Mary [Appleton], May 29, 1863, Appleton Scrapbook, 9, WVU; Schouler, *History of Massachusetts in the Civil War,* 409–10; Emilio, *Brave Black Regiment,* 33.

CHAPTER 25. SOUTH CAROLINA

1. John [Appleton] to Mary [Appleton], May 29, 1863, Appleton Scrapbook, 8–9, 11–12. James Gooding reported that one man jumped overboard on the first night at sea, *New Bedford Mercury,* June 19 (2:3), 1863. RGS to John Andrew, June 5, 1863, in *Annual Report of the Adjutant-General of Massachusetts of the Commonwealth of Massachu-*

setts . . . for the Year Ending Dec. 31, 1863 (Boston: Wright & Potter, 1864), 58.

2. RGS to AHS, June 1, 1863, SHAW, 291.

3. Maj-Gen David Hunter to Col Shaw, June 3, 1863, "Special Orders," Department of the South, Record Group 393, NA; Maj-Gen [David] Hunter to E. M. Stanton, June 3, 1863, and Maj-Gen [David] Hunter to John Andrew, June 3, 1863, *OR*, 1:14, 462−63; *Report of Adjutant-General, 1863,* 900; John [Appleton] to Mary [Appleton], June 5 and 7, 1863, Appleton Scrapbook, 13−17.

4. RGS to John Andrew, June 5, 1863, *Report of Adjutant-General, 1863,* 58.

5. *BECF,* 346n.

6. Thomas W. Higginson, *Army Life in a Black Regiment* (1869; reprint, New York: W. W. Norton, 1984), 216; *BECF,* 340n.

7. Maj-Gen [David] Hunter to Col W. H. Davis, June 6, 1863, "Registers of Letters Sent," Dept. of the South, Record Group 393, NA; Appleton Scrapbook, 20; Morning Reports of June 9 and 10, Bound Volumes, 54th Mass. Inf. (Colored), Records of the Adjutant General's Office, Record Group 94, NA.

CHAPTER 26. BURNING GEORGIA

1. RGS to FGS, June 5, 1863, RGS to SBS, June 6, 1863, RGS:COLL.

2. RGS to AHS, June 9, 1863, SHAW, 296−97; *BECF,* 346n.

3. RGS to AHS, June 12, 1863, SHAW, 297.

4. Ibid.; Appleton Scrapbook, 22−23; Report of Capt. W. G. Thomson, June 13, 1863, and Report of Capt. W. A. Lane, June 19, 1863, *OR* 1:14, pp. 318−19; newspaper clipping, June 16, 1863, in Hallowell Papers, MHS; E. Merton Coulter, "Robert Gould Shaw and the Burning of Darien, Georgia," *Civil War History* 5 (Oct. 1959): 363−65; J. W. Grace to Gen. Peirce, June 14, 1863, Camp Meigs Papers, NBFPL.

5. RGS to FGS, May 27, 1862, RGS:COLL; John [Appleton] to Mary [Appleton], June 11, 1863, Appleton Scrapbook, 24; RGS to AHS, June 9, 1863, SHAW, 341−44; Charles Lowell to ES, June 20, 1863, and Charles Lowell to William Whiting, June 26, 1863, in Emerson, *Life and Letters of Lowell,* 261−62, 265−67.

6. *Savannah News,* June 16, 1863, quoted in *Boston Commonwealth,* July 3 (4:3), 1863; newspaper clipping, *NYDT,* June 24, 1863, in Hallowell Papers, MHS; Emilio, *Brave Black Regiment,* 383; newspaper clipping, *New Bedford Mercury,* July 8, 1863, in Scrapbook of James Bunker Congdon, Soldiers' Fund Committee, NBFPL.

7. RGS to AHS, June 12, 1863, SHAW, 298; RGS to SBS, June 29, 1863, RGS:COLL.

8. Frederick Douglass, "The Burning of Darien," newspaper clipping in Hallowell Papers, MHS; *Boston Commonwealth,* July 3 (2:3, 3:3–4), 1863; RGS to Governor [John A.] Andrew, June 14, 1863, *Annual Report of Adjutant-General, 1863,* 59.

9. Emilio, *Brave Black Regiment,* 43–44; Burchard, *One Gallant Rush,* 110–11; James, "Assault upon Fort Wagner," 15; *OR,* 1:28.

10. RGS to SBS, June 13 and 28, 1863, RGS:COLL; RGS to Charley [Lowell], June 20, 1863, NYPL.

11. Special Order No. 13, June 13, 1863, Special Order No. 16, June 16, 1863, Special Order No. 19, June 19, 1863, and Daily Call Order, June 28, 1863, Bound Volumes, 54th Mass, Record Group 94, NA; Cabot [Russel] to Father, June 14 and 21, 1863, Russell Papers, NYPL; J. W. Grace to Gen [R. A.] Peirce, June 14, 1863, Camp Meigs Papers, NBFPL; Appleton Scrapbook, June 18 and 22, 1863, 26–27.

12. RGS to AHS, June 26 and 27, 1863, RGS to SBS, June 28, 1863, *SHAW,* 309–10, 312; RGS to Charley [Morse], July 3, 1863, MHS; RGS to Mary Forbes, June 7, 1862, RGS:COLL.

CHAPTER 27. FANNY KEMBLE AND CHARLOTTE FORTEN

1. RGS to AHS, June 28, 1863, SHAW, 310; RGS to SBS, June 28, 1863, RGS:COLL.

2. James, "Assault upon Fort Wagner," 15. Appleton Scrapbook, June 18, 1863, 27; Gooding quoted from *New Bedford Mercury,* June 30 (2:3), 1863; J. W. Grace to [R. A.] Peirce, June 14, 1863, Camp Meigs Papers, NBFPL; RGS to ES, June 15, 1863, SHAW, 349.

3. RGS to AHS, June 9–13, 1863, RGS to SBS, June 13, 1863, SHAW, 296–301, 302.

4. RGS to SBS, June 6, 1863, RGS:COLL; Ray Allen Billington, ed.,

The Journal of Charlotte L. Forten (New York: Dryden Press, 1953), 10–16, 25; *BECF,* 375n.

   5. RGS to SBS, July 3–6, 1863, SHAW, 315–18; Billington, *Journal of Charlotte Forten,* 211–13.

   6. Billington, *Journal of Forten,* 212–213; RGS to SBS, July 4, 1863, SHAW, 316; Dorothy Sterling, ed., *We Are Your Sisters: Black Women in the Nineteenth Century* (New York: W. W. Norton, 1984), 279–82.

   7. Billington, *Journal of Forten,* 213–14; RGS to SBS, July 6, 1863, SHAW, 316.

CHAPTER 28. THEY FOUGHT LIKE HEROES

   1. RGS to SBS, June 28, 1863, RGS:COLL.; RGS to George C. Strong, July 6, 1863, quoted in Smith, *Beacon Hill's,* 441.

   2. RGS to Governor [John A.] Andrew, July 2, 1863, in Emilio, *Brave Black Regiment,* 47–48; Appleton quoted in *Commonwealth,* July 24 (3:2), 1863.

   3. RGS to FGS, July 1, 1863, RGS:COLL.; *BECF,* 367n.

   4. Emilio, *Brave Black Regiment,* 47–48; the best source for details on Gillmore's operation against Charleston is *OR,* 1:28.

   5. RGS to AHS, July 9–13 and 13, 1863, SHAW, 322–24, 325; Emilio, *Brave Black Regiment,* 53–63; Cabot [Russel] to Father, July 14, 1863, Russell Papers, NYPL.

   6. *NYDT,* July 27 (1:1), 1863; *New Bedford Mercury,* Aug. 8 (2:3), 1863.

   7. RGS to AHS, July 15, 1863, SHAW, 325–26. In the excitement of the fight, Shaw probably misdated this letter—should be July 16; Cabot [Russel] to Father, July 18, 1863, Russell Papers, NYPL; Appleton letterbook, WVU; soldier in Tenth Connecticut quoted in Glatthaar, *Forged in Battle,* 136; Bowen, *Massachusetts in the War,* 674.

   8. RGS to AHS, July 15, 1863, SHAW, pp. 325–26; *BECF,* 387n.

CHAPTER 29. THE GRAND OPPORTUNITY

   1. RGS to AHS, July 17, 1863; Appleton letterbook, WVU; Morning Reports, July 16 and 17, 1863, Regimental Order Book, 54th Massachusetts, Bound Volumes, Records of the Adjutant General's Office, Record Group 94, NA; Emilio, *Brave Black Regiment,* 63–65.

2. Emilio, *Brave Black Regiment*, 65−68.

3. Appleton Papers, WVU; *NYDT*, July 27 (1:2−4), 1863; Seymour quoted in the Testimony of Nathaniel Paige, in Berlin, *Black Military Experience*, 534; *OR*, 1:28, pt. 1, 362; Edward L. Pierce described the regiment as "worn and weary," *National Anti-Slavery Standard*, Aug. 8 (1:5−6), 1863; James, "Assault upon Fort Wagner," 20.

4. *Memorial: RGS*, 151, Hallowell quoted on 165−66; Burchard, *One Gallant Rush*, 34−35; Emilio, *Brave Black Regiment*, 67.

CHAPTER 30. FORT WAGNER

1. Pierce recalled his last meeting with Shaw: "I parted with Colonel Shaw as he rode to join his regiment. As he was leaving, he turned back and gave me his letters and other papers, telling me to keep them and forward them to his father if anything occurred," Higginson, *Soldier's Book;* Emilio, *Brave Black Regiment*, 73−78; Luis F. Emilio, "The Assault on Fort Wagner" (Boston: Rand Avery, 1887), 8−9; J. W. M. Appleton, "That Night at Fort Wagner," *Putnam's Magazine* 19 (July 1869): 13; Appleton letterbook, WVU; Gooding letter in *New Bedford Mercury*, Aug. 29 (2:2), 1863.

2. *NYDT*, July 31 (3:4−5), 1863; *New Bedford Mercury*, Aug. 29 (2:2), 1863; a black soldier's remembrance in Josephine Lowell to AHS Shaw, July 9, 1882, Stewart, *Philanthropic Works*, 63−64; Grace quoted from *New Bedford Standard*, July 29 (2:2), 1863; *Charleston Daily Courier*, July 20 (1:3−5), 1863; Robert C. Gilchrist, *The Confederate Defence of Morris Island, Charleston Harbor* (Charleston: News & Courier, 1884), 18; James, "Assault upon Fort Wagner," 21−22.

3. *National Anti-Slavery Standard*, Aug. 8 (1:5−6), 1863; *OR*, 1:28, pt. 1, pp. 210, 279; Testimony of Nathaniel Paige, in Berlin, *Black Military Experience*, 535; Johnson Hagood, *Memoirs of the War of Secession* (Columbia, S.C.: The State Company, 1910), 1:142−43; newspaper clipping no. 594 in Hallowell Papers, MHS; letter of John Luck in Higginson, *Soldier's Book*, n.p.

4. James, "Assault upon Fort Wagner," 23−26; Appleton letterbook, WVU.

5. Lewis [Douglass] to Amelia [Loguen], 20 July 1863, Carter Woodson Papers, LC.

6. *National Anti-Slavery Standard,* Aug. 1 (3:5), 1863; Emilio, *Brave Black Regiment,* 105–27, 386; A. S. Fisher to My Dear Aflicted Captin [George Pope], July 31, 1863, Albanus S. Fisher Papers, Gettysburg College; Surgeon Stone to Governor Andrew, July 24, 1863, in *Annual Report of the Adjutant-General, 1863,* 59–61; Billington, *Journal of Forten,* 193–96; Laura Towne, *Letters and Diary of Laura M. Towne: Written from the Sea Islands of South Carolina, 1862–1864* (1912; reprint, New York: Negro Universities Press, 1969), 115.

7. Exslave quoted from Yacovone, *Voice of Thunder,* 46; Billington, *Journal of Forten,* 213–17.

CHAPTER 31. AFTERMATH: FIFTY-FOURTH MASSACHUSETTS INFANTRY

1. Emilio, *Brave Black Regiment,* 106–8.

2. Ibid., 120.

3. Ibid., 279, 393–433; James, "Assault upon Fort Wagner," 23, 27; General Order No. 252, July 31, 1863, *OR* 2:6, p. 163.

4. Emilio, *Brave Black Regiment,* 148–216, 277–88, 310–14.

5. Ibid., 227–28, 317–20.

6. Ibid., 330, 336; Glatthaar, *Forged in Battle,* 140, 152, 179.

CHAPTER 32. AFTERMATH: SHAW'S FAMILY

1. Charles Lowell to ES, July 28, 1863, and Charles Lowell to Harry Russell, July 26, 1863, in Emerson, *Life and Letters of Lowell,* 285, 288; Edward L. Pierce to SBS and FGS, July 22, 1863, in *Memorial: RGS,* 54; Meltzer and Holland, *Lydia Maria Child,* 433.

2. FGS to Edward L. Pierce, July 31, 1863, FGS to Dr. Stone, Aug. 3, 1863, Francis George Shaw Letters, HL; William Vaughn Moody, "An Ode in Time of Hesitation," in *The Columbia Book of Civil War Poetry: From Whitman to Walcott,* ed. Richard Marius (New York: Columbia University Press, 1994), 130.

3. See Ogden [Haggerty] to Charles P. Haggerty, July 24, 1863, in Robert Gould Shaw: Military and Personal Telegrams, NYHS; Burchard, *One Gallant Rush,* 147; and "Topics of the Time," *Century Magazine* 54 (June 1897): 312.

4. Stewart, *Philanthropic Works,* 28, 30, 37; *In Memorium: Josephine*

Shaw Lowell (New York: Charity Organization of New York, 1905), 43–101; James B. Lane, "Jacob A. Riis and Scientific Philanthropy During the Progressive Era," *Social Science Review* 47 (March 1973): 32–48; Lowell's letter quoted in Ferris Greenslet, *The Lowells and Their Seven Worlds* (Boston: Houghton Mifflin, 1946), 294.

5. See "Notes on the Barlow Family" by Louisa Barlow Jay, Barlow Collection, HL.

6. SBS to John E. Cairnes, November 2, 1863, quoted in Adelaide Weinberg, *John Elliot Cairnes and the American Civil War: A Study in Anglo-American Relations* (London: Kingswood Press, 1969), 167.

7. SBS to Rev. [Robert] Clute, August 29 and September 24, 1870, quoted from Buddy Sullivan, *Early Days on the Georgia Tidewater: The Story of McIntosh County and Sapelo* (Darien, Ga.: Darien News, 1990), 305–6.

8. FGS to Edwin M. Stanton, 6 October 1863, Records of the Office of the Secretary of War, RG 107, Micro. 221, Roll 240, Letter S-1361, NA; McPherson, *Struggle For Equality,* 189; ES to Charles Eliot Norton, Dec. 31, 1902, as quoted in Waugh, "Unsentimental Reformer," 101n.

CHAPTER 33. GLORY

1. *Atlantic Monthly* quoted from Lader, *Bold Brahmins,* 290; Anna Mary Wells, *Dear Preceptor: The Life and Times of Thomas Wentworth Higgninson* (Boston: Houghton Mifflin, 1963), 180; *Boston Commonwealth,* July 31 (3:1), 1863; *Richmond County Gazette,* Aug. 19 (2:5), 1863; W. E. B. Du Bois, *Black Reconstruction in America: An Essay Toward a History of the Part Which Black Folk Played in the Attempt to Reconstruct Democracy in America, 1860–1890* (New York: Atheneum, 1935), 110.

2. Emilio, *Brave Black Regiment,* 229; E. N. Hallowell to Rufus Saxton, October 7, 1864, N. P. Hallowell Papers, MHS; Towne, *Letters and Diary,* 116; for the best look at Saint Gaudens and the poems to Shaw, see Saint-Gaudens, *Reminiscences;* Steven G. Axelrod, "Colonel Shaw in American Poetry: 'For the Union Dead and Its Precursors,'" *American Quarterly* 24 (October 1972): 523–37; and Robert Lowell, *"Life Studies" and "For the Union Dead"* (New York: Noonday Press, 1971).

3. Emilio, *Brave Black Regiment,* 391.

4. Charles Sumner to E. L. Pierce, July 29, 1863, in Edward L. Pierce, ed., *Memoirs and Letters of Charles Sumner* (Boston: Roberts Brothers, 1877–1893), 4:142; Allen Flint, "Black Response to Colonel Shaw," *Phylon* 45 (Fall 1984): 210–19; Axelrod, "Colonel Shaw," 523–37.

5. Quoted in Axelrod, "Colonel Shaw," 525.

6. J. R. Lowell, "Memoriae Positum: R.G.S., 1863," in RGS:COLL.

7. Lowell, *Life Studies,* 70–72.

8. Orations of William James and Booker T. Washington at Shaw Memorial, May 31, 1897, quoted from Richard Benson, *Lay This Laurel* (New York: Eakins, 1973), n.p.

SELECTED BIBLIOGRAPHY

MANUSCRIPTS

Boston Public Library

    Lydia Maria Child Papers.

    William Lloyd Garrison Papers.

    Thomas W. Higginson Papers.

    Massachusetts Infantry, Second Regiment. Letters from the Army: A Scrapbook.

    Weston Sisters Papers.

Gettysburg College Library

    Albanus S. Fisher Papers.

Houghton Library, Harvard University

    George William Curtis. Papers, 1842–1892.

    Henry Lee Higginson scrapbook: "The Soldier's Book."

    Louisa Barlow Jay Collection.

    Amos Adams Lawrence Papers.

    Francis George Shaw Letters.

    Robert Gould Shaw Collection.

    Sarah Blake Sturgis Shaw Papers.

    Frank Vizetelly. Sketches.

Massachusetts Historical Society

    John Albion Andrew Papers.

    Nathan Bowditch. CDV album: "Our Martyr Soldiers of the Great Rebellion." Broadsides-L. (1863).

    Carte-de-Visite Album, Civil War, Fifty-fourth Massachusetts.

    Richard Cary Papers.

    Crowninshield-Magnus Papers, 1834–1965.

Dana Collection: Letter, Francis G. Shaw to George Ripley, Feb. 1845.

Fifty-fourth Massachusetts Infantry Regiment Papers.

Norwood P. Hallowell Papers and Scrapbooks, 1764–1914.

A. A. Lawrence Collection.

Lee Family Papers.

James Russell Lowell Papers, 1842–1924.

T. Lyman III Collection.

Lyman Family Papers, 1785–1956.

Miscellaneous Bound.

Photographic Collection.

MS.L. Robert Gould Shaw.

R. G. Shaw II Collection.

National Archives

Record Group 94. Records of the Adjutant General's Office.

Bound Record Books. Second Massachusetts Infantry.

Bound Record Books. Fifty-fourth Massachusetts Infantry (Colored).

Colored Troops Division, 1863–1889.

Compiled Military Service Records.

"The Negro in the Military Service of the United States, 1607–1889."

Pension Files.

Record Group 107. Records of the Office of the Secretary of War.

Letters Received.

Record Group 393. Department of the South.

Letters Received.

Registers of Letters Sent.

Special Orders.

New Bedford Free Public Library

Camp Meigs Papers.

Soldier's Fund Committee. Scrapbook of James Bunker Congdon.

New York Historical Society

Robert Gould Shaw. Military and Personal Telegrams.

Shaw folder. Photograph of Robert Gould Shaw.

New York Public Library, Rare Books and Manuscripts Division

Cabot Jackson Russel. Papers, 1859–1865.

Shaw Family Letters, 1862–1876.

Staten Island Historical Society

George William Curtis clippings.

Shaw family folder.

F. G. Shaw House photograph.

Staten Island Institute of Arts and Sciences

George William Curtis Collection.

F. G. Shaw, biographical notes.

United States Army Military History Institute at Carlisle Barracks

George L. Andrews Papers.

Massachusetts-MOLLUS Collection.

West Virginia University Library

John W. M. Appleton Papers, 1861–1916. Letterbook.

BOOKS AND ARTICLES

Adams, Virginia M., ed. *On the Altar of Freedom: A Black Soldier's Civil War Letters from the Front.* Amherst: University of Massachusetts Press, 1991.

Amory, Cleveland. *The Proper Bostonians.* New York: E. P. Dutton, 1947.

Annual Report of the Adjutant-General of the Commonwealth of Massachusetts . . . for the Year Ending December 31, 1863. Boston: Wright & Potter, 1864.

Appleton, J. W. M. "That Night at Fort Wagner." *Putnam's Magazine* 19 (July 1869): 9–16.

Aptheker, Herbert, ed. *A Documentary History of the Negro People of the United States.* 2 vols. New York: Citadel Press, 1951.

———. *The Negro in the Civil War.* New York: International Publishers, 1938.

Axelrod, Steven G. "Colonel Shaw in American Poetry: 'For the Union Dead' and Its Precursors." *American Quarterly* 24 (October 1972): 523–37.

Bartlett, Samuel R. *The Charge of the Fifty-fourth.* Chicago: Church, Goodman & Donnelly, 1869.

Bayles, Richard M., ed. *History of Richmond County (Staten Island) New*

York from Its Discovery to the Present Time. New York: L. E. Preston, 1887.

Benson, Richard. *Lay This Laurel: An Album on the Saint-Gaudens Memorial on Boston Common Honoring Black and White Men Together Who Served the Union Cause with Robert Gould Shaw and Died with Him July 18, 1863.* New York: Eakins, 1973.

Berlin, Ira, et al. *Freedom: A Documentary History of Emancipation, 1861–1867.* Series I, *The Destruction of Slavery.* Cambridge: Cambridge University Press, 1985.

Berlin, Ira, Joseph P. Reidy, and Leslie S. Rowland, eds. *Freedom: A Documentary History of Emancipation, 1861–1867.* Series II, *The Black Military Experience.* Cambridge: Cambridge University Press, 1985.

Billington, Ray Allen, ed. *The Journal of Charlotte L. Forten.* New York: Dryden Press, 1953.

Blassingame, John W., ed. *The Frederick Douglass Papers.* 3 vols. New Haven, Conn.: Yale University Press, 1979–85.

Blight, David W. *Frederick Douglass' Civil War: Keeping Faith in Jubilee.* Baton Rouge: Louisiana State University Press, 1989.

Bowen, James L. *Massachusetts in the War, 1861–1865.* Springfield, Mass.: Bryan, 1889.

Brown, Francis Henry. "First Report of the Class of 1857 in Harvard College." Cambridge, Mass.: John Wilson & Sons, 1866.

———. *Harvard University in the War of 1861–65.* Boston: Cupples, 1886.

———. *Report of the Class of 1857 in Harvard College.* Cambridge, Mass.: John Wilson, 1893.

———. "Roll of Students of Harvard University Who Served in the Army or Navy of the United States During the War of the Rebellion." Cambridge, Mass.: Welch, Bigelow, 1866.

Brown, William Wells. *The Negro in the American Rebellion: His Heroism and His Fidelity.* New York: Lee & Shepard, 1867.

Browne, Albert G. *Sketch of the Official Life of Governor Andrew.* New York: Hurd & Houghton, 1868.

Burchard, Peter. *One Gallant Rush: Robert Gould Shaw and His Brave Black Regiment.* New York: St. Martin's Press, 1965.

Cairnes, John E. *The Slave Power: Its Character, Career, and Probable Designs; Being an Attempt to Explain the Real Issues Involved in the American Contest.* New York: Carleton, 1862.

Cary, Edward. *George William Curtis.* Boston: Houghton Mifflin, 1894.

A Catalogue of the Officers and Students of Harvard University for the Academical Year 1856–57 . . . 1858–59. 6 pamphlets. Cambridge, Mass.: John Bartlett, 1856–1858.

Child, Lydia Maria. "Correspondence between Lydia Child and Gov. Wise and Mrs. Mason of Virginia." In *Anti-Slavery Tracts.* Boston: American Anti-Slavery Society, 1860. Reprint, Westport, Conn.: Negro Universities Press, 1970.

———. *Letters of Lydia Maria Child.* Boston: Houghton Mifflin, 1882.

Clark, Emmons. *History of the Seventh Regiment of New York, 1806–1889.* 2 vols. New York: Published by the author, 1890.

Clute, J. J. *Annals of Staten Island, from Its Discovery to the Present Time.* New York: Charles Vogt, 1877.

Cooke, George W. *Unitarianism in America: A History of Its Origin and Development.* Boston: American Unitarian Association, 1902.

Cornish, Dudley T. *The Sable Arm: Negro Troops in the Union Army, 1861–1865.* New York: Longmans, 1956.

———. "To Be Recognized as Men: The Practical Utility of History." *Military Review* 58 (February 1978): 40–55.

Coulter, E. Merton. "Robert Gould Shaw and the Burning of Darien, Georgia." *Civil War History* 5 (Fall 1959): 363–73.

Crawford, Mary C. *Famous Families of Massachusetts.* 2 vols. Boston: Little, Brown, 1930.

Curtis, George William. *From the Easy Chair.* 3 vols. New York: Harper, 1892.

Dalzell, Robert. *Enterprising Elite: The Boston Associates and the World They Made.* Cambridge, Mass.: Harvard University Press, 1987.

Dictionary of American Biography. 10 vols and 8 suppls. New York: Charles Scribner's Sons, 1927–88.

Du Bois, W. E. B. *Black Reconstruction: An Essay Toward the History of the Part Which Black Folk Played in the Reconstruction of America.* New York: Harcourt, Brace, 1935.

Duberman, Martin B. *James Russell Lowell*. Boston: Houghton Mifflin, 1966.

Duncan, Russell, ed. *Blue-Eyed Child of Fortune: The Civil War Letters of Colonel Robert Gould Shaw*. New York: Avon Press, 1994.

Dwight, Elizabeth, ed. *Life and Letters of Wilder Dwight, Lieut-Col. 2nd Massachusetts Infantry Volunteers*. Boston: Ticknor & Fields, 1868.

Emilio, Luis F. *A Brave Black Regiment: History of the Fifty-fourth Regiment of Massachusetts Volunteer Infantry, 1863–1865*. Boston: Boston Book Co., 1891. Reprint, New York: Arno Press, 1969.

———. *The Assault on Fort Wagner*. Boston: Rand Avery, 1887.

Flint, Allen. "Black Responses to Colonel Shaw." *Phylon* 45 (Fall 1984): 210–19.

Foner, Eric. *Free Labor, Free Soil, Free Men: The Ideology of the Republican Party Before the Civil War*. New York: Oxford University Press, 1970.

———. *Politics and Ideology in the Age of the Civil War*. New York: Oxford University Press, 1980.

Foote, Shelby. *The Civil War: A Narrative*. New York: Random House, 1958–74.

Forbes, Abner, and J. W. Greene. *The Rich Men of Massachusetts*. Boston: Fetridge, 1852.

Forten, Charlotte. "Life on the Sea Islands." *Atlantic Monthly* 13 (May 1864): 587–96, 13 (June 1864): 666–76.

Fox, William F. *Regimental Losses in the American Civil War, 1861–1865*. Albany, N.Y.: Albany Publishing Co., 1889.

Frederickson, George M. *The Black Image in the White Mind: The Debate on Afro American Character and Destiny, 1817–1914*. New York: Harper & Row, 1971.

———. *The Inner Civil War: Northern Intellectuals and the Crisis of the Union*. New York: Harper & Row, 1965.

Garrison, W. P., and F. J. Garrison. *William Lloyd Garrison, 1805–1879: The Story of His Life*. 4 vols. New York: Century, 1889.

Gerteis, Louis S. *From Contraband to Freedman: Federal Policy Toward Southern Blacks, 1861–1865*. Westport, Conn.: Greenwood Press, 1973.

Gilchrist, Robert C. *The Confederate Defence of Morris Island, Charleston Harbor.* Charleston, S.C.: News & Courier, 1884.

Gladstone, William A. *United States Colored Troops, 1863–1867.* Gettysburg, Pa.: Thomas Publishers, 1990.

Glatthaar, Joseph T. *Forged in Battle: The Civil War Alliance of Black Soldiers and White Officers.* New York: Free Press, 1990.

Gordon, George H. *History of the Second Massachusetts Regiment of Infantry.* Boston: Alfred Mudge & Son, 1874.

Gray, J. Glenn. *The Warriors: Reflections of Men in Battle.* New York: Harper & Row, 1959.

Greenslet, Ferris. *The Lowells and Their Seven Worlds.* Boston: Houghton Mifflin, 1946.

Hallowell, Norwood P. *The Negro as a Soldier in the War of the Rebellion.* Boston: Little, Brown, 1897.

———. *Selected Letters and Papers of N. P. Hallowell.* Peterborough, N.H.: Richard R. Smith Co., 1963.

Hampton, Vernon B. *Staten Island's Claim to Fame.* Staten Island, N.Y.: Richmond Borough, 1925.

Harvard College. *Report of the Class of 1860: 1860–1866.* Cambridge, Mass.: Wilson & Sons, 1866.

Headley, Phineas C. *Massachusetts in the Rebellion.* Boston: Walker, Fuller, 1866.

Heller, Charles E. "The 54th Massachusetts." *Civil War Times Illustrated* 11 (April 1972): 32–41.

———. "George Luther Stearns." *Civil War Times Illustrated* 13 (July 1974): 20–28.

Higginson, Henry Lee. *Four Addresses.* Boston: Merrymount Press, 1902.

Higginson, Mary T., ed. *Letters and Journals of Thomas Wentworth Higginson, 1846–1906.* Boston: Houghton Mifflin, 1921.

Higginson, Thomas W. *Army Life in a Black Regiment.* 1869. Reprint, New York: W. W. Norton, 1984.

———. *Cheerful Yesterdays.* 1899. Reprint, New York: Arno Press, 1968.

———. *Harvard Memorial Biographies.* 2 vols. Cambridge, Mass.: Sever & Francis, 1867.

————. *Massachusetts in the Army and Navy During the War of 1861–65.* 2 vols. Boston: Wright & Potter, 1896.

————. "The Shaw Memorial and the Sculptor St. Gaudens." *Century Magazine* 54 (June 1897): 176–200.

Hine, Charles G., and William T. Davis. *Legends, Stories and Folklore of Old Staten Island.* New York: Staten Island Historical Society, 1925.

Horton, James O., and Lois E. Horton. *Black Bostonians: Family Life and Community Struggle in the Antebellum North.* New York: Holmes & Meier, 1979.

Hughes, Sarah Forbes, ed. *Letters and Recollections of John Murray Forbes.* 2 vols. Boston: Houghton Mifflin, 1899.

James, Garth W. "The Assault upon Fort Wagner." In *War Papers Read before the Commandery of the State of Wisconsin, Military Order of the Loyal Legion of the U.S.* Milwaukee: Burdick, Armitage & Allen, 1891.

Kaplan, Sidney. *American Studies in Black and White.* Amherst: University of Massachusetts Press, 1990.

Kemble, Frances Anne. *Journal of a Residence on a Georgian Plantation in 1838–1839.* Edited, with an introduction, by John A. Scott. New York: Knopf, 1961. Reprint, Athens: University of Georgia Press, 1984.

King, Spencer B., Jr. *Darien: The Death and Rebirth of a Southern Town.* Macon, Ga.: Mercer University Press, 1981.

Lader, Lawrence. *The Bold Brahmins: New England's War Against Slavery in 1831–1863.* New York: E. P. Dutton, 1961.

Lane, James B. "Jacob A. Riis and Scientific Philanthropy During the Progressive Era." *Social Science Review* 47 (March 1973): 32–48.

Langston, John M. *From the Virginia Plantation to the National Capitol.* Hartford: American Publishing Co., 1894. Reprint, New York: Johnson Reprint Corp., 1968.

Leng, Charles W., and William T. Davis. *Staten Island and Its People: A History, 1609–1929.* 2 vols. New York: Lewis Publishing Co., 1929–30.

Linderman, Gerald F. *Embattled Courage: The Experience of Combat in the American Civil War.* New York: Free Press, 1987.

Lowell, Robert. *"Life Studies" and "For the Union Dead."* New York: Noonday Press, 1971.

Massachusetts Soldiers, Sailors, and Marines in the Civil War. 8 vols. Norwood, Mass.: Norwood Press, 1931.

McFeely, William S. *Frederick Douglass.* New York: W. W. Norton, 1991.

————. *Grant: A Biography.* New York: W. W. Norton, 1981.

McKay, Ernest A. *The Civil War and New York City.* Syracuse, N.Y.: Syracuse University Press, 1990.

McPherson, James M. *Battle Cry of Freedom: The Civil War Era.* New York: Oxford University Press, 1988.

————. *For Cause and Comrades: Why Men Fought in the Civil War.* New York: Oxford University Press, 1997.

————. *The Negro's Civil War: How American Negroes Felt and Acted During the War for the Union.* New York: Pantheon, 1965.

————. *The Struggle for Equality: Abolitionists and the Negro in the Civil War and Reconstruction.* Princeton, N.J.: Princeton University Press, 1964.

Meltzer, Milton, and Patricia Holland, eds. *Lydia Maria Child: Selected Letters, 1817–1880.* Amherst: University of Massachusetts Press, 1982.

Meltzer, Milton, ed. *The Black Americans: A History in Their Own Words, 1619–1983.* New York: Harper & Row, 1964.

Memorial: RGS. Cambridge, Mass.: Harvard University Press, 1864.

Merrill, Walter M., and Louis Ruchames, eds. *The Letters of William Lloyd Garrison.* 7 vols. Cambridge, Mass.: Harvard University Press, 1979.

The Monument to Robert Gould Shaw: Its Inception, Completion and Unveiling, 1865–1897. Boston: Houghton Mifflin, 1897.

Morse, Charles F. "From Second Bull Run to Antietam." In *War Papers and Personal Reminiscences, 1861–1865.* St. Louis: Becktold, 1892.

————. *Letters Written During the Civil War, 1861–1865.* Boston: Privately printed, 1898.

Nalty, Bernard C. *Strength for the Fight: A History of Black Americans in the Military.* New York: Free Press, 1986.

Nalty, Bernard C., and Morris J. MacGregor. *Blacks in the Military: Essential Documents.* Wilmington: Scholarly Resources, 1981.

Oakey, Daniel. *History of the Second Massachusetts Regiment of Infantry: Beverly Ford, June 9, 1863.* Boston: George H. Ellis, 1884.

Oates, Stephen B. *To Purge This Land with Blood: A Biography of John Brown.* New York: Harper & Row, 1970.

Pearson, Elizabeth W., ed. *Letters from Port Royal, 1862—1868.* New York: Arno Press, 1969.

Perry, Bliss, ed. *Life and Letters of Henry Lee Higginson.* Boston: Atlantic Monthly Press, 1921.

Pickard, John B., ed. *The Letters of John Greenleaf Whittier.* 3 vols. Cambridge, Mass.: Harvard University Press, 1975.

Pierce, Edward L., ed. *Memoir and Letters of Charles Sumner.* 4 vols. Boston: Roberts Brothers, 1877—93.

Putnam, Elizabeth C., comp. *Memoirs of the War of '61: Colonel Charles Russell Lowell, Friends, and Cousins.* Boston: G. H. Ellis, 1920.

Quarles, Benjamin. *The Negro in the Civil War.* Boston: Little, Brown, 1953. Reprint, New York: Da Capo, 1989.

Quint, Alonzo Hall. *Record of the 2nd Massachusetts Infantry.* Boston: James P. Walker, 1867.

Record of the Massachusetts Volunteers, 1861—1865. 2 vols. Boston: Wright & Potter, 1870.

Record of the Service of the Fifty-fifth Regiment of Massachusetts Volunteer Infantry. 2 vols. Cambridge, Mass.: John Wilson & Son, 1868.

Redding, Saunders. "Tonight for Freedom." *American Heritage* 9 (June 1958): 52—55, 90.

Roehrenbeck, William J. *The Regiment That Saved the Capital.* New York: A. S. Barnes, 1961.

Rose, Willie Lee. *Rehearsal for Reconstruction: The Port Royal Experiment.* New York: Oxford University Press, 1964.

Saint-Gaudens, Homer, ed. *The Reminiscences of Augustus Saint-Gaudens.* 2 vols. New York: Century, 1913.

Scharnhorst, Gary. "From Soldier to Saint: Robert Gould Shaw and the Rhetoric of Racial Justice." *Civil War History* 34 (December 1988): 308—22.

Schouler, William. *A History of Massachusetts in the Civil War.* 2 vols. Boston: E. P. Dutton, 1868.

Shaw, Frances George. "A Piece of Land." In *Social Problems,* by Henry George. New York: J. W. Lovell, 1883.

Shaw, Robert Gould. *Letters: RGS.* Cambridge, Mass.: Harvard University Press, 1864.

————. *Letters: RGS.* New York: Collins & Brother, 1876.

————, trans. *The Children of the Phalanstary: A Familiar Dialogue on Education,* by F. Cantagrel. New York: W. H. Graham, 1848.

Smith, Marion W. *Beacon Hill's Colonel Robert Gould Shaw.* New York: Carlton Press, 1986.

Souvenir of the Massachusetts Fifty-fourth (Colored) Regiment. Boston: N.p., 1863.

Sterling, Dorothy, ed. *We Are Your Sisters: Black Women in the Nineteenth Century.* New York: W. W. Norton, 1984.

Stewart, James Brewer. *Holy Warriors: The Abolitionists and American Slavery.* New York: Hill & Wang, 1976.

Stewart, William R. *The Philanthropic Works of Josephine Shaw Lowell.* New York: Macmillan, 1911.

Stowe, Harriet Beecher. *The Key to Uncle Tom's Cabin.* Boston: Jewett, 1854. Reprint, New York: Arno Press, 1968.

Sturgis, Roger Faxton, ed. *Edward Sturgis of Warmouth, Mass., 1613–1695, and His Descendants.* Boston: Stanhope, 1914.

Swift, Lindsay. *Brook Farm: Its Members, Scholars, and Visitors.* New York: Macmillan, 1900.

Swinton, William. *History of the Seventh Regiment National Guard, State of New York, During the War of the Rebellion.* New York: Dillingham, 1886.

Teamoh, Robert T. *Sketch of the Life and Death of Colonel Robert Gould Shaw.* Boston: Boston Globe, 1904.

"Topics of the Time." *Century Magazine* 54 (June 1897): 312–14.

Towne, Laura. *Letters and Diary of Laura M. Towne: Written from the Sea Islands of South Carolina, 1862–1884.* 1912. Reprint, New York: Negro Universities Press, 1969.

Trow's New York City Directory for the Year Ending May 1, 1860 [1861–1863]. New York: John F. Trow, 1859 [1860–1862].

Twiggs, Hanaford D. D. *Defence of Battery Wagner, July 18, 1863.* Augusta, Ga: Chronicle Publishing Co., 1892.

United States Census. Eighth Census. 1860. New York, Richmond County.

The War of the Rebellion: A Compilation of the Official Records of the Union and Confederate Armies. 128 vols. Washington, D.C.: U.S. Government Printing Office, 1880–1901.

Waugh, Joan. "Unsentimental Reformer: The Life of Josephine Shaw Lowell." Ph.D. dissertation, University of California–Los Angeles, 1992.

Weinberg, Adelaide. *John Elliot Cairnes and the American Civil War: A Study in Anglo-American Relations.* London: Kingswood Press, 1969.

Wells, Anna Mary. *Dear Preceptor: The Life and Times of Thomas Wentworth Higginson.* Boston: Houghton Mifflin, 1963.

Werstein, Irving. *The Storming of Fort Wagner: Black Valor in the Civil War.* New York: Scholastic Books, 1970.

Whitehall, Walter M. *Boston and the Civil War.* Boston: Boston Athenaeum, 1963.

Whitman, Robert Shaw Sturgis. "The 'Glory' Letters." *Berkshire (Mass.) Eagle,* February 2(6:2), 1990.

Williams, George W. *A History of Negro Troops in the War of the Rebellion, 1861–1865.* New York: Harper, 1888. Reprint, New York: Greenwood Press, 1969.

Wilson, Joseph T. *The Black Phalanx: A History of the Negro Soldiers of the United States in the Wars of 1775–1812, 1861–'65.* Hartford: American Publishing Co., 1888. Reprint, New York: Arno Press, 1968.

Yacovone, Donald, ed. *A Voice of Thunder: The Civil War Letters of George E. Stephens.* Urbana: University of Illinois Press, 1997.